ANIMALS IN COMBAT

ANIMALS IN COMBAT

Nigel Allsopp

NEW HOLLAND

This book is dedicated to my mum Doreen.

Little of size but big of heart,

I am truly blessed to have her as my mum during this journey of life.

Animals in War monument in London's Hyde Park

Contents ★>>>

Introduction ✪》》

During thousands of years of global conflict animals have served alongside man in warfare. But what makes them useful in war? A dog's qualities of loyalty, intelligence and devotion are highly valued in their role as pets, and these traits are also very attractive to the armed forces. Equines such as horses, mules and donkeys have literally carried man and military supplies on their backs. Among their many duties, animal warriors have also carried messengers through trenches, or flown over them. They have carried ammunition, medical equipment and our wounded. Finally they have given us physical and emotional comfort and aided moral.

Sadly thousands of animals have been left on enemy shores to unknown fates as troops sailed home after the conflicts. This has happened to troops from all countries, but is outlined in several touching poems from Australian Light horsemen during World War I. Many of these soldiers went and shot their own mounts, rather than risk a selection board that posted category-A horses as remounts to such places as India, but gave lesser-quality horses to the locals they suspected would work them to death. This was just a fraction of the number of casualties in that conflict; over the duration of World War I it has been estimated that more than 8 million animals were killed or wounded.

My own research even estimates this amount is far too low. By the end of the war, Russia was a Soviet state and no information has ever been officially released. For that matter, it is unknown as to how many war animals were lost by that country alone. I suspect like figures from World War II, Russia may have lost several million more combat animals.

Despite World War II being regarded as a mechanised conflict, millions of animals were used by all sides and again millions gave the ultimate sacrifice.

In developing countries, animals are still used as a means of transport. This may be due to inaccessible roads or routes that can only be used by four-legged transport; or simply poverty.

Since ancient times, combat has involved a variety of animals from insects and bacteria used in biological warfare to the better known war horse. Camels, carrier pigeons, elephants, mules, donkeys, bats, dogs and even bees have all been used in combat in some form.

Hannibal crossed the Alps with large numbers of elephants 2,200 years ago to battle the Romans. These pachyderms died in droves as the general from Carthage forced them over the range, while the Romans only accounted for a few of their deaths during the ensuing battles.

Pigeons performed messenger missions in World War I and World War II. Some 200,000 pigeons served the colours over both conflicts and suffered huge losses. Recently, Coalition troops Iraq used the birds as chemical-warfare detectors. They served by dying, alerting troops of a chemical attack.

Even glow worms have served in the military; soldiers during World War I sometimes smashed them on their helmets to act as a night time identification signal to friendly forces. Needless to say the casualty rate was significant.

Today, military working dogs are the animal most likely to be used in combat. However marine mammals and equines still play an important role, with the latter undergoing a major resurgence in Afghanistan. Coalition forces, including the US, Britain and Australian Special Forces have used locally scoured horses and mules as transport and pack animals in the wild terrain of Afghanistan and the border areas of Pakistan's North-West frontier. One positive aspect of this has been the training of the soldiers in animal-management and basic veterinary techniques. Thus while operating in tribal areas the soldiers have won the hearts and minds of locals by treating their sick farm animals.

Service animals are those that work for humans doing a particular task. These tasks may be as mundane as hauling ammunition or as sophisticated as locating an underwater mine. The common factor is that service animals help humans' needs. Some people see this as a clever use of resources and a mutual beneficial bond, while others see it as a form of slavery. Some animal-rights activists believe animals should not be used by man at all, where others say its okay for such work as guide dogs or law enforcement.

One of the first great civilisations to put animals to work was the ancient Egyptians. They used a variety of animals mainly donkeys, oxen, camels and horses for transportation, beasts of burden and war. All of these animals can be found somewhere in the world doing the same thing today.

The use of animals by the military is controversial; these animals are often put into tremendous danger and many have died during their service. On the other hand many of the military and my own observations have seen service animals saved countless lives, whether it be by locating a roadside bomb or carrying a wounded soldier to a field hospital.

The following chapters explore a brief history of military animals throughout the ages, their different roles within this period, what animal warriors are used for today and what future animals have in modern warfare. One wish of mine writing this book is that whatever your opinion, that next holiday dedicated to soldiers who gave their lives in war, please pause a thought for the four-legged heroes that fought and died alongside them. Hopefully one day we can not only stop sending our pets to war, but our sons and daughters, too.

Acronyms
ADF - Australian Defence Force
AWAMO - Australian War Animal Memorial Organization
USMC - United States Marine Corps
USAF – United States Air Force
ADFTWDA - Australian Defence Force Trackers and War Dog Association

POEM

I don't think I could stand the thought of my old fancy hack
Just crawling round old Cairo with a 'Gyppo on his back.
Perhaps some English tourist out in Palestine may find
My broken-hearted Waler with a wooden plough behind.

No: I think I'd better shoot him and tell a little lie:--
"He floundered in a wombat hole and then lay down to die."
May be I'll get court-martialled; but I'm damned if I'm inclined
To go back to Australia and leave my horse behind.

From an Australia in Palestine, 1919

Photograph courtesy of the Australian Light Horse Association

Lieutenant Dennis Wheatly describes the high casualty rate of horses on the front lines in 1915: "There were dead ones laying all over the place and scores of others were floundering and screaming with broken legs, terrible neck wounds and their entrails hanging out. We went back for our pistols and spent the next hour putting the poor seriously injured brutes out of their misery by shooting them through the head. To do this we had to wade ankle deep through blood and guts. That night we lost over 100 horses."

Brigadier General Frank Percy Crozier observed at the battle of the Somme: "If the times are hard for human beings on account of the mud and misery which they endure with astounding fortitude, the same may be said for the animals. My heart bleeds for the horse and mules."

Chapter 1:
Animals at War Today ★》》

This photo above could have been taken during World War I, but the uniforms give it away. In 2012, US forces used animals in much the same way their great grandfathers did. Photograph courtesy of USMC (Photograph courtesy of by Staff Sgt. Robert M. Storm)

Many roles that animals have performed in ancient times have, thankfully, become redundant in modern conflicts. However, animals such as horses, donkeys and mules still conduct much the same vital role today as they did serving the armies of Rome. Advances in training and animal physiology have also opened up new uses for animals such as marine mammals and canines in modern warfare.

Some animals used in ancient times are being looked at again to help man; even snakes. In ancient times armies rounded up poisonous snakes, crated them in baskets and launched them over enemy siege walls. This was a type of psychological warfare more to terrify residents and soldiers, and in reality did not actually kill many people. Today US scientists are studying snakes' heat-sensing abilities to improve detection equipment and give combat troops the edge.

Biological warfare using animal by-products is not a modern tactic; the earliest recorded use in 1500-200 BC was by the Hittites. Scythian soldiers in 400 BC used snake venom, human blood and animal faeces on their arrows to infect wounds. Two thousand years later the Vietnamese were doing the same thing to bamboo sticks laid for unsuspecting GIs.

Animal-borne bombs

Some animals have been used in the past to attack and kill man directly, in Roman and Greek times, pigs were used not only to terrify elephants with their squeals the larger animals hated, but the same poor animals were drenched in oil, set alight and driven towards the mass elephant ranks. Not surprisingly the elephants bolted in terror. Elsewhere, straw was attached to the back of camel and set alight before a charge with much the same results. Many elephants would turn and crush their own troops in an attempt to avoid the noise and smoke.

Most people would agree this is barbaric, but sadly even in modern times humans used animals in a similar suicide role. The Russians trained hundreds of dogs strapped with explosive charges to run under German tanks in World War II. This was done by starving the dogs for days then feeding them only under a tank. Once the dog got the idea that it was fed under a tank, they would strap it with a live device and take it to the front. The device was initiated when the dog's harness, containing an antenna, connected with the metal of the tank's belly, resulting in an explosion. The Russians eventually gave up the idea when several dogs turned around ran under Soviet tanks instead. It seems one tank looks and smells much the same to a starving dog.

Sadly, such practices have manifested in other forms even today in war in

Afghanistan and Iraq. There have been several incidences since 2004 of donkeys and mules being loaded with explosives and set off at US and Israeli check points throughout the Middle East. The increase by terrorist groups caused the President of PETA, an animal's rights group, to formally approach Yasser Arafat asking him to keep animals out of the conflict.

The process alas still continues with animals being used as late as 2009 by the Taliban, which strapped explosives to a donkey and detonated it as it approached a Coalition camp and hospital.

Battle Bees

Despite their small size, bees can be an effective weapon. The ancient Greeks, Romans and other civilisations occasionally used these insects as tiny weapons to deter enemy forces from occupying an area. It works this way by placing bee hives in dead ground where you cannot see the enemies approach. It denies the enemy by using this same ground. If the bees are disturbed you can see their movement or hear the painful yell of a soldier. In siege warfare, hives were catapulted over walls. Upon hitting the ground, they burst open releasing a swarm of angry stinging animals which took their displeasure out on the nearest victim. It was not just the sting in the tail that can be a weapon, the Trabzon tribe in Turkey tricked the Roman soldiers under the command of Pompey with a tribute of toxic honey, causing vomiting and stomach pains prior to the battle. This had a devastating effect on the Romans' ability to fight. During World War I and as late as Vietnam, bees were used as bobby traps and as early warning systems against approaching troops similar to ancient times.

Bat Bombs

One of the most hare-brained ideas of using animals in warfare must go the US Army, which attempted to train thousands of Mexican free-tailed bats to become suicide bombers in World War II. The bat bomb idea was conceived by a dental surgeon called Lytle Adams. He submitted his idea to the White House in 1942 where amazingly it was approved by the President himself.

The inventor of military napalm, Louis Fieser designed a 17-gram incendiary device that could be carried by a bat.

The plan was to fly B24 bombers over enemy territory from a base in Alaska, each carrying 100 bomb-shaped casings containing 40 bats, each with one of Fieser's timed incendiary bombs attached to its leg. The casings containing the bats would be dropped at dawn at 1500 metres, the casing would then deploy a parachute in mid-flight and release the bats. It was thought that, as the sun rose, the bats would automatically seek dark places such as eaves and attics to roost in. Then the inbuilt timer would ignite the bombs, causing wide spread fires in the predominantly wood-and-paper constructed houses and factories of Japanese cities.

But when a practical test phase was undertaken however in the US, indiscriminate bats managed to set fire to not just the mock Japanese village but several hangers, US chemical factories and a general's car. Then the next phase of testing found all the bats in the B24 at altitude froze to death before reaching the target.

Thankfully the war ended and the bats were not operationally use. Today these flying mammals are being studied again, this time to see if their flight mechanics can improve future spy robot design. Likewise the similar study of an insect's natural motion is helping develop the next generation of micro spy robots which can enter an area unseen and transmit information.

Carrier Pigeons ★>>

Pigeons have been used to communicate information in wars for thousands of years, and they have even been highly decorated for their bravery. Photograph courtesy of Bob Whithouse, Military heritage museum

The first historical mention of the pigeon being used to carry messages in war was in the city of Sumer in southern Mesopotamia in 2500 BC. It is said the ruler of the city released two doves to carry the news the city was freed from warring neighbours.

The homing and navigational skills of the carrier pigeon has made these birds heroes of both world wars. The Allies used as many as 200,000 pigeons during World War I. One of these birds, Cher Ami, earned the French "Crois de Guerre" for delivering lifesaving messages after being shot through the eye and leg by German sharpshooters at the battle of Verdun.

Many other pigeons during both world wars were awarded the Dickins Medal for bravery and heroism. The Dickins Medal is considered the equivalent of the Victoria Cross for animals and is awarded to an animal that has distinguished itself through an act of bravery in wartime. Of the 55 medals awarded to date, 32 have been given to pigeons.

Two Australian pigeons have won the Dickins medal; both in World War II. One bird flew to Madang to saved the crew and valuable cargo of a vessel that was floundering during a tropical storm. In driving rain, the bird covered 64 kilometres in 50 minutes and by the end of the war had been on 23 missions. The other medal went to an Australian pigeon attached to the US Forces on Manus Island north of New Guinea in April 1944. A group of some 200 troops were tied down by superior Japanese forces, suffering growing causalities. But they managed to release a pigeon carrying a plea for help. The bird arrived back at base some 48 kilometres away in just 47 minutes. Aircraft were sent to clear the area and the troops were saved certain death or captivity.

For some people who visit places such as Time Square, London's Trafalgar Square or the local park, pigeons can seem to be a pest; rats with wings. They have however saved the lives in war of thousands of soldiers.

In 2004 an impressive memorial to commemorate all the animals killed during wartime was erected in Hyde Park, London. Pigeons have been given pride of place on the wall in a carved relief.

A General in World War I stated:

It is the pigeon on which we must and do depend when every other method fails. During quiet we can rely on the telephone, telegraph, flag signals and various other ways in use on the front, but when the battle rages and everything gives way to barrage and machine gun fire to say nothing of gas attacks and bombing, it is to the pigeon that we turn too. When the troops are lost or surrounded in the mazes on the front, or are advancing and yet beyond known causalities, then we depend absolutely in the pigeon for our communications. Regular methods in such cases are worthless and it is just such times that we need most messengers that we can rely on. In pigeons we have them. I am glad to say that they have never failed us.

During the D-Day invasion of World War II, Allied soldiers maintained radio silence and relied on pigeons to send messages back to headquarters in England notifying them of the landings success. Pigeons continued to be used throughout Europe and as far afield as Burma and India. The American and Australian forces used birds extensively and had their own pigeon units operating in many different countries.

Sending messages by pigeon also saved on precious airtime, as war correspondents came to appreciate and removed the need for decoding. But perhaps most valuable of all, no radio had yet been invented that could transmit a map or hastily sketched drawing of an enemy position.

Allied bomber crews carried a pair of pigeons so that, in the event the plane was shot down the birds could be released with details of the location of the crash site. One example of this was on February 1942 when a Beauford bomber had to ditch into the sea off the Norwegian coast after being damage during a raid. One of the pigeons managed to escape from its container after the damaged aircraft had broken up upon crashing. The bird managed to travel 270 kilometres back to its base, covered in oil from the damaged plane, and deliver its message. Subsequently the crew were rescued.

Pigeons were not only used as messengers, Project Pigeon was an attempt to develop a bird-guided missile. Sound like the bat bomb idea with similar results if it worked for the life of the pigeon. The pigeon was placed inside a missile complete with a warhead. The idea was the bird was trained through food reward to peck at the centre of a picture of a German ship. If the missile started to go off course the pigeon would tap on the screen and the missile would come back on track. There was one major fault; the pigeons could not tell the difference between a German or Allied ship.

Thankfully the project was cancelled for this reason, but was revived again by the US Navy in 1948 as project Orcon. It was cancelled again in favour of electronic guidance systems by 1953.

Pigeons had a remarkable record of success as messengers but they did not have everything their own way. A bounty was given to any soldier who shot an enemy pigeon. Since it was also an offence to shoot one of your own birds, we're not sure how successful this option was. The Germans trained falcons and hawks—the peregrine falcon is one of the world's fastest animals—to attack pigeons in the air. .

The pigeon's role in intelligence cannot also be underestimated. Pigeons were used to maintain contact with resistance fighters across Europe, often flying over enemy territory where they stood a better chance of getting a message delivered than an aircraft. In 2005, MI5 released a wartime secret documents that revealed that from prisoners of war they had found out German pigeons would be used to convey information obtained by agents in England. To counter this, MI5 set up its own crack force of peregrine falcons with the aim of felling enemy pigeons. The MI5 falcons were set up over the Scilly Isles after reports of pigeons disappearing towards France. These falcons would patrol for several hours at a time, attacking any pigeon which flew near the area. According to documents in the Public Records Office, at least two enemy pigeons became prison over the islands of the Cornish coasters of war. Displaying typical military humour, the report further stated that were now working hard at breeding English pigeons.

Birds of prey are still used by the Belgian Air Force, which has a specialist unit of raptors trained to kill and ward off birds from military airfields. Today these birds scare off flocks which otherwise might cause aircraft crashes.

It is not surprising some have considered a comeback of the war pigeon. They can fly 125 kilometres per hour unaffected by today's electronic jamming systems. Today modern armies such as China, Israel and France still maintain a pigeon capability. France still maintains around 150 birds in the 8th Communications Regiment, stationed west of Paris. The Swiss army reserve owns around 7,000 pigeons and pays private owners to maintain 24,000 more for possible operational service. The birds have been tested to cover 800 kilometres carrying messages, tape recordings and microfilm. An automatic miniature camera has been tested that mounts via a canvass harness around the bird; the pigeon flies over a strategically important area to capture images. This is not a new concept and a similar attempt to mount cameras on pigeons was tried during World War II with only limited success making them in effect the first Unmanned Ariel Vehicles—UAVs.

Of course today UAVs are large platforms for a mass of instruments and fly thousands of metres in the sky to avoid detection. Interestingly, the US Army are developing the NANO Hummingbird system where mini UAVs are designed to look like small birds rather than machines. It has a camera incorporated into its body and flies low and fast like the real hummingbird spying on enemy positions. Other bird look alike are under development to suit various habitats. Watch out next time you are out at Sea, that seagull maybe a mini naval spy drone.

Chapter 2:
The War Donkey ⭐⟫⟫

Photograph courtesy of graphs supplied by Giovanna Devlin

Right up to this century, few wars could have been fought without the donkey. In one campaign alone in East Africa during World War I, 34,000 donkeys were used to support British troops. By the time the campaign ended just three weeks later only 1,042 donkeys were still alive, thanks to tsetse fly infestation.

France and Italy deployed many donkeys during World War I. Italy alone used some 100,000 in their Alpine battles. France in turn used around the same number on the Western Front carrying up to 90 kilograms of supplies at a time to the trenches.

ANZAC troops also used thousands of donkeys usually obtained in-situ from allied or local sources. However, if you have ever tried to Google 'Australian war donkey' you would be forgiven for thinking country used only one; called Murphy and associated with the ANZAC tradition of Gallipoli.

Murphy was one of the most famous donkeys is the one used by John Simpson Kirkpatrick to fetch wounded ANZAC troops down from the hilly front lines to the medical stations on the beach. Simpson would start his day at 0600 hours and continue sometimes until 0300 hours the next day. He made this two-and-a-half kilometre trip through sniper fire at least 12-15 times a day. Simpson wound leave his donkeys under cover (there is a myth that it was just Murphy but in fact Simpson used several donkeys—one being called Duffy and a number of others) while he went forward to collect the injured then the donkeys would carry the men down the hill. On their return journey they would carry fresh water back up the hill.

Although now legendary, this act of bravery lasted only 24 days until Simpson was killed. He was recommended for the Victoria Cross twice and the Distinguished Conduct Medal, but they were never awarded. Murphy the donkey received the RSPCA's Purple cross as a hero.

Padre George Green at Simpson's burial service said:
> "If ever there was a man deserve the Victoria Cross it was Simpson. I often remember now the scene I saw frequently in shrapnel Gully, of that cheerful soul calmly walking down the gully with a Red Cross armlet tied round the donkey's head. That gully was under direct fire from the enemy almost all the time."

Sgt. Hookway, his Section Sergeant, said of him:
> "a big man and very muscular, though aged only 22 and was selected at once as a stretcher bearer... he was too human to be a parade ground soldier, and strongly disliked discipline; though not lazy he shirked the drudgery of 'forming fours', and other irksome military tasks."

Despite Simpson's lack of official decorations he has been enshrined in ANZAC history having pictures of himself and Duffy on everything ranging from stamps to the Australian 100 dollar bill. Perhaps the commemorative that most represents this team was a simple stone that replaced the cross on his grave at Gallipoli, it reads:

JOHN SIMPSON
KIRKPATRICK SERVED AS
202 PRIVATE
J SIMPSON,
AUST. ARMY MEDICAL CORPS,
19TH MAY 1915 AGE 22
HE GAVE HIS LIFE
THAT OTHERS MAY LIVE.

Interestingly today the motto "that others may live" is the official unit motto of the United States Air Forces elite para-rescue medic in Afghanistan.

As for Duffy, Murphy and the other donkeys; no-one really knows exactly what happened to them. There have been several stories. Some say the Indian Muleteers, who Simpson loaded the donkeys off in the first place took them back upon the Allied withdrawal. Other sources state they were killed, as were many hundreds at Gallipoli. Another source states an Indian army ambulance officer, fearing donkeys were being shot or left to the Turks, hung a luggage label around his halter saying "Murphy VC please look after him". Murphy may have been recognized by ANZAC troops and taken to France or Egypt. Finally one children's book says he was last seen eating grass on the island of Lemnos were some of the donkeys were recruited from. The truth is we will probably never know what happened.

That of course was not the end to the war donkey. During World War II all nations, Axis and Allied, relied on donkey transportation in areas as diverse as Crete to the jungles of Burma.

War donkeys were again to be seen in 1973 when the British Army fought with Omani forces against leftist guerrillas. They used the animals in a logistical role, climbing narrow tracks and hills that trucks could not negotiate. Often the donkeys would be transported themselves by trucks from bases to the foot of the mountains, where they then would take over carrying the kit. They were used a few years later by the British Special Forces in Aden, Yemen, in much the same role.

In fact the donkey and special forces would begin a partnership that still exists today. British, US and Australian special forces teams can be seen high up in the mountains with an old-fashioned donkey carrying the latest sophisticated satellite communications equipmen or the team's 81 mm mortar.

The Canadian Army, for example, already have tanks, armoured vehicles and helicopters at their disposal in their battle against the Taliban. But they also added 30 donkeys to their arsenal as beasts of burden recently. The previous time Canadian troops used donkeys was during World War II in Sicily.

The terrain in the sector where the Canadian troops operate today is particularly difficult to negotiate with modern means of transport. The area contains mountains, rivers, irrigation canals, walled compounds and wadis. The area's few roads are very narrow.

The donkeys are used to supplement the load-carrying capacity of the soldiers in an area where temperatures can reach searing heights. They can carry a significant amount of weight up to 160 kilograms. This gives the Canadians an ability to deliver, via pack animals, vital supplies such as water and ammo to places where mechanised or aviation assets cannot reach.

The donkeys used by coalition forces in Afghanistan also have another positive spin to the local community. For example, most are purchased locally from tribal leaders and stimulate the economy. Locally purchased animals are used to the local terrain, local food, and weather.

Secondly, instead of a tank breaching a village command wall to pass through, a donkey train can walk around.

It's not just special forces or organised regiments that use donkeys. It's not unusual for an enterprising soldier raised on a farm to enlist a local equine in the rugged mountain terrain for the occasional task. After all Osama bin Ladin rode one, why not his pursuers?

The donkey has a special place in my heart from riding them as a kid on the beaches in Broadstairs, England were I was born, to as a New Zealand serviceman riding them on an ANZAC day race against Turkish UN troops in the UNSOM camp, Mogadishu, Somalia. Finally to marching with them on parades in my home of Australia were they usually have pride of place in war animal ceremonies.

There are still around 44 million donkeys in the world today, mainly doing what they have done for the last 6,000 years; pulling carts, or transporting man or supplies on their backs.

We have not seen the last of the war donkey.

Chapter 3:
Combat Mules ⭐》》

Pfc. Vahram A. Terzikyan, an infantry assault man with Weapons Company, 3rd Battalion, 4th Marine Regiment, and Pfc. Scotty D. Couch, an anti-tank missile man with Weapons Company, 3/4, guide the way for their mules during a training exercise of the animal packers course offered by the Marine Corps Mountain Warfare Training Center Bridgeport, Calif., near Hawthorne Army Ammunition Depot training grounds in Hawthorne, Calif., Feb. 25. Photograph courtesy of By: Cpl. Nicole A. LaVine

Mules are perhaps the most underrated and unappreciated animal to serve the colours. Perhaps more mules have given the ultimate sacrifice to man than any other animal, yet sadly there are very few military monuments to honour them.

A mule is the product of the union between a female horse and a male donkey, whereas a hinny is the union of a male horse or pony with a female donkey. This latter breed is usually not used by the military as they are rare—it seems male horses don't fancy female donkeys as much as a donkey will fancy your mare, which has no problem mating outside its species. Secondly, and perhaps more importantly, a hinny is physically weaker and smaller. Mules vary in size depending on what mare you cross the donkey with—by using a draught horse, the resulting mule inherits the larger animal's size and strength.

The military mule is used for riding, heavy draught work, as a pack animal or towing wagons. Their working life can be as long as 20 years, they can walk 65 kilometres a day at an average pace of 5km/h, carrying loads of up to 200 kilograms. Terrain and environment will alter these figures—a mule operating in the jungle at night will be limited to what the handler, known as a muleteer, can manage. With the exception of deep snow, a mule can traverse any terrain. As a rule, a mule can climb a slope a man can without the use of his hands.

As good as mules are, there are some pros and cons in using them in the military. They can be quite vocal— no good if trying to ambush the enemy. However, there is a least one recorded occasion when an Allied force was surrounded and vastly outnumbered by the Japanese in the jungle, the mules made such a noise that the Japanese in turn thought a major force was about to attack them and fled.

They can also be fussy drinkers, preferring to go thirsty rather than drink from an unfamiliar stream. Yet they would drink the same water if you put it in its own bucket. A military commander must therefore plan the route taken by the mule train to accommodate this factor. In World War I, it was recorded that a column of mules in Palestine, having trekked 65 kilometres, were so desperate for water, one mule broke loose and jumped down a well. It took several hours to extricate the mule and dozens of soldiers to prevent other mules trying to join it.

Mules can be trained to tolerate battlefield noise and, when used on the front lines, tend to need one muleteer per animal. In a support role, one muleteer can handle up to half a dozen animals.

Mules have always been a vital part of any military campaign, carrying everything an army needs. The ancient Roman legions marched with one mule for every 10 legionnaires. Napoleon himself rode a mule across the Alps, not as pictured on his famous white stallion. He also used them in his baggage trains. The US military has used mules in combat since the Black Hawk Wars of 1832 and again in the Seminole War of 1835-1842.

By the Mexican War in the mid-1840s the US Army used mules to pull supply wagons, ambulances and as pack animals. During the Spanish-American war more than 3,000 mules were used in Florida. Again, during the American Civil War, mules were depended upon to transport artillery and supplies, leaving horses for the cavalry. The Union army alone used more than a million mules, in just one campaign at Chattanooga 75,000 mules were deployed by General Sherman. The Confederacy on the other hand used half as many mules and most soldiers had to supply their own. Many of these were taken from farms and it is speculated by some historians that the shortage of mules directly contributed to the South's ultimate defeat due to their effect on farm production and the economy.

So important were they to the war effort President Lincoln when reviewing Union troops is said to have paid more attention to the comfort of the mules than of the officers.

Mules can be surprisingly affectionate and loyal, not at all the stubborn beast many think. Photograph courtesy of Cpl. Nicole A. LaVine

The US has always been a supplier of mules to not only its own military but across the world. During the Zulu war of 1879, Britain brought thousands of mules from North America. Again in World War I, 275,000 mules were supplied to Britain's Expeditionary Forces. When America herself joined World War I, the US army required 571,000 mules in Europe. About 68,000 of those were killed in action and many more wounded.

Many people think of the sinking of the *Lusitania* in 1915 as the key factor that caused the US to end its neutrality. Yet the second ship sunk by German U-Boat that week was the straw that broke the camel's back. The *SS Armenian* was owned by the White Star Line—of *Titanic* fame—and was torpedoed off Cornwall, England. It was a mule-transport vessel containing more than 1,400 mule teams and their African-American muleteers. Such was the value of mules no quarter or warning shots were given—at this stage of the war some chivalry on the high seas still existed—and all 1,400 mules drowned along with about 78 muleteers.

Muleteers themselves are often regarded as secondary troops in many armies and relegated to support roles only. Many armies did not even issue them weapons. It was even a job for slaves from ancient times right up to the American Civil War. They were, however, a vital component to any campaign and the cry to recruit handlers went out during World War I.

The British got a boost to their mule service from two distinct areas. One was the Zion Mule Corps, formed in 1914 to aid the war against the Ottoman Empire. Many Jews from around the world saw an opportunity to promote the idea of a Jewish homeland and signed up. For political reasons, the British opposed their participation on the Palestine front, so out of the 650-strong Zion Mule Corps all but around 90 were sent to Gallipoli.

As Turkey had joined the Central Powers, the status quo concerning the occupation of Cyprus by Turkey caused Britain to ally with Greek Cypriots. The military Commander of the British Divisions in Saloncia formally requested a formation of an Army Corps of muleteers which he considered essential to fight the Germans and Bulgarians in the mountainous region of Macedonia. By the summer of 1916, Cypriot muleteers in Salonika numbered 9200. By 1919 the number of this forced reached 15,910 men, while the population of Cyprus according to a census at the time was only 150,000. Some 30 Cypriot muleteers were killed in action between 1916 and 1919.

In World War II, the British Lancashire Fusiliers in the Tunisian mountains used mules rather than Bren gun carriers or lorries to deliver supplies. These mules were loaded with jerry cans and were also fitted with special litters to carry the wounded. Again in mainland Italy and Sicily, pack mules were used in the medical evacuation role by the 9th US Medical Battalion to bring numerous cases of trench foot out from the front lines. Many problems were reported such as the rough ride and exposure to fire due to the mules' high profile. But the mule could go where even a jeep could not and so were used where conditions demanded it. This same method of medical evacuation had been re-evaluated and US troops in some remote mountainous environments of Afghanistan are being evacuated out by mule today.

Like donkeys, mules in both World War II and present times would have been purchased locally.

Many people believed their day was over as the last active service mules— Trotter and Hambone—in the US Army were retired in 1956. Not so. The mule is making a strong comeback in the US, this time with the Marines. A mule operator school has been established at the Marine Mountain Warfare Training Center in California for Marines heading off to Afghanistan. This two-week course is designed to teach equine husbandry and how to pack animals with gear for operations in the mountains of Hindu Kush, where most Afghans live. So effective has this course been, now special forces from various countries undertake this course. Ironically this course is a revamp of a packer's course developed in 1981 for CIA agents being sent to Afghanistan.

Not to be outdone by the Marines, the US Army still has a few mules at the US Military Academy West Point, where selected cadets use them at sporting events and public relations parades a tradition that dates back to 1899. The choice of a mule as a mascot reflects the long standing usefulness of this animal in military operations, hauling guns, supplies and troops. Strong, hearty and persevering the mule is an appropriate symbol for the Corps of Cadets.

If the army will not issue soldiers with the right tools, they have the habit of acquiring them. During the Korean War, the famous Wolf Hound Regiment had 33 mules as part of their machine gun unit. Many other nations used mules in this war, usually obtained by various ways from locals or the enemy.

So valuable were mules, troop commanders were reluctant to inform headquarters if they had captured mules for fear they would be taken from them. On one operation the 1st Cavalry Division moved mules they had acquired by trucks to the mountainous sector north of Seoul to the Imjin River. The captured mules were used to pack items such as barbed wire, steel stakes and mines. Interestingly one of these captured animals was a former American mule whose brand 08K0 identified him as one of many mules shipped to China during World War II and later commandeered by the Red Army.

Other countries that still use mules today include Argentina, Germany, Austria, Switzerland and France. The French Foreign Legion is famed for using mules as part of their desert flying columns and has used them and other animal transport on operations in Chad and Somalia as recently as 2001. So useful is the mule that man has tried to replace it by mechanical inventions. First there has been various 6x6 logistic buggies that carry twice the load of a mule but can only traverse half the ground the animal can.

To counter this the US Army is spending millions on a remote-controlled mechanical mule. Just like a mule, it has four legs but is prone to fall over. It still needs a man to operate it and is perhaps a decade away from being perfected. When asked what the end result will be a NASA spokesman said it should be able to do anything a mule can do. Is it just me or does that not make any sense at all; why not just use a $100 mule? It reminds me a bit of the NASA project that reputedly spent billions on a space pen that was able to write in zero gravity, while the Russians spent 50 cents on a pencil.

Chapter 4:
War Camels ⭐》》

Well before the invention of the engine, Arabs found camels indispensable in the desert climates of North Africa and the Middle East. The first recorded military use of war camels was at least 1200 BC. However, it wasn't until between 500-100 BC that bactrian camels finally attained military use. The bactrian is a two-humped camel found in Asia and ideal for working in hard cold climates. The Chinese and Russian armies still use them in remote inhospitable areas such as the Gobi Desert.

However, the dromedary single-humped camel is the favoured military animal used for both military transport and to carry mounted troops. Arab warriors used camels during the Muslim conquests, while the British officer known as Lawrence of Arabia utilised them with great effect during World War I. They continue to find a military function to this day.

Having the advantages of speed and maneuverability over other animals, camels are ideal for surprise attacks in desert conditions. Unlike a horse-mounted cavalry soldier who remains mounted after charging up to the enemy, camel troops usually dismount and fight as infantry.

It is not just the Arabs that have made use of the camel in war. In 1884 a British camel corps was formed for the Gordon Relief expedition to the Sudan and again in 1915 the Camel Brigade—later the Imperial Camel Corps—made up of British, Indian, Australian and New Zealand troops was raised for action in the Middle East.

Despite the widescale use of motor transport in areas where the terrain permitted it, the British forces operating in the Middle East and the 1919 Afghan war still relied on camel pack columns for their supplies. The British used camels in the British Somaliland as patrol platforms until 1960.

The Spanish army used Sahrawi tribesman as auxiliary camel mounted troops in the Sahara from 1930 until the end of Spanish presence in the territory in 1975. Apart from being ridden, they were also used to carry supplies and provided meat, wool, milk and fuel in the form of their dry dung to the soldiers.

Today the Indian Army's Border Security Force—BSF—plans to send some 60 combat trained camels to solve the transport headache facing the fledgling UN African Union peacekeeping force in Sudan's strife-torn Darfur region.

The BSF uses 700 camels to conduct long-range reconnaissance, night and patrols to help track down drug smugglers heading across their boarders from Pakistan. Camels are ideal; not only can they sustain patrols for long periods of time at up to 60 km/h, they don't require you to empty your wallet at a petrol station. The South African Defence Force also operates full-time camel units.

I have worked with camels at various zoos and they can be aggressive and stubborn. But once trained, I can see how effective a military mount they would be. They have wide feet, enabling them to spread their body weight while crossing soft sand. A camel can carry 200 kilograms for 32 kilometres a day. A camel can endure 10 days without water and can endure thirst and hunger with little complaint, so much so that incidents have occurred that a rider only knew his camel was at its limit as it dropped down dead.

Military attributes also include being generally docile under fire and a tendency not to panic. One handler can lead a string of up to eight camels; over poorer terrain it is cut back to two animals. In war, various contraptions have been developed for camels to carry stores and casualties. One such device is the cacolet, where two patients are carried either side of the camel in a type of suspended stretcher. A much better system was to use two camels in unison to make a versatile cross-country litter called a charpoy.

Chapter 5:
War Elephants ★》》

I was privileged to work with Asian elephants for several years as a trainer and keeper at the Auckland Zoo. I later went onto work with African elephants at Western Plains Zoo in Australia. I know from firsthand experience what these intelligent and strong animals can do. It is not surprising that military forces throughout time have harnessed their strength and imposing looks for the battlefield.

Elephants are a cohesive, socially orientated family herd animal without a hint of aggression unless that group is threatened. I believe they were not so much trained to be vicious on the battlefield but rather expected to perform certain functions that could cause death and injury to enemy soldiers. I have trained elephants to pick up people, head standing and stomping on objects such as containers to get food out. All these actions, if so trained, could be used on a battlefield to kill people.

Their sheer size was usually enough to intimidate the approaching force; by simply walking forward they would sweep all before them.

War elephants were trained to stamp on soldiers and impale them on their tusks. But they could also carry out engineering projects such as clearing vegetation, hauling trees to build bridges or carrying heavy equipment.

Although African elephants can be trained, the Indian elephant has a far longer tradition of service to mankind. It was however the African elephant that crossed the Alps with Hannibal.

Elephants were usually recruited locally in the many wars in what is now India. Here the earliest known military application was around 1100 BC. It is uncertain when the first elephant were used by Europeans in battle, but Alexander the Great first encountered them during his campaigns and eventually their use was spread to the Greeks, Carthaginians and Romans, where any self-respecting general had to have them in his order of battle. Even though they were more of a gimmick than a tactical advantage, the elephant decided the fate of many battles in the Greek and Roman periods.

Psychological warfare has always been a part of war from the earliest of times till now and the war elephant certainly played its part in this role. Image how terrifying it must have been to hear, see and smell this giant beast running at you at 40 km/h on the field of battle if you had never seen one before. A fully mature Indian elephant can weigh 5,000 kg. Many German soldiers during World War I would have felt the same when the elephant's modern-day equivalent, the tank broke through their trenches. Likewise, what a morale-booster if they were on your side.

Like the modern tank, elephants depend on mobility, firepower and protection. Archers were mounted in wicker baskets atop the elephant's back and rained arrows down on the infantry below. The animal itself provided the mobility whilst its body was often protected by chain mail and plates.

It was common to use females. While males were larger and more aggressive, they would have a condition called musth which is marked by an oil-like secretion from glands behind the eye. When in musth, the animal's only aim is to mate and it becomes uncontrollable. In effect, it is then useless in battle.

Even so with female elephants, accidents, either designed by the enemy or the result of panic, can turn the tide of a battle. The elephant's power is based on force and at 40 km/h can trample an enemy line easily. However, they are also difficult to stop. Some have panicked and turned around, crushing their own forces.

Eventually elephants fell out of favour on the battlefield due to them being difficult to source and expensive to maintain—the average mature female can eat 225 kilograms of fodder a day and drink 90 litres of water.

They were loaned from zoos and used in World War I to haul heavy equipment in both British and German munitions factories. The Indian Army used them in both world wars in the transport and logistics role right up to the 20th century. India used elephants to move guns and supplies as recently as 2010 and they assisted in engineering projects during recent civil disasters. Even in the US, Special Forces Field manual's 2004 edition lists elephants as a viable pack animal.

There are plenty of military purposes elephants could still be used, in countries where they are native. During the 2010 emergencies in Myanmar and Thailand, they were used to aid civil power during the earthquakes and monsoon flooding. In developing countries, the armed forces maybe gave a saving grace to the endangered elephant by giving them a home and employment. Elephants in these regions are traditionally accepted and respected. They are ideal engineering assets, being all-terrain mobile bulldozer, haulage truck, chainsaw and plough system all in one. Their fuel is also plentiful and free.

Chapter 6:
The Horse ⭐⟩⟩

Photograph courtesy of Kedron/Wavell RSL

1st Cavalry Division's Horse Cavalry Detachment charge during a ceremony at Fort Bliss, Texas, 2005.

It seems for as long as men have fought one another they have done so on horseback. The death of the cavalry has been declared many times. When the British archers annihilated the French nobility at the battle of Agincourt, who sank under the weight of their own armour many said their day was gone. When the French Cuirassiers could not break the British squares at Waterloo, the cavalry was said to be history.

As far as a frontal attack on well-prepared troops, the mounted charge has probably been obsolete since the days of the Swiss pike formation, the English longbow men and the rifled musket. The introduction to the infantry of the machine gun was thought to have gotten rid of the notion of a cavalry charge.

But like so many things that people claim are old-fashioned or out of date, the cavalry kept on finding a role for themselves. Right up to World War II, cavalry units were in every major power's order of battle. The Americans charged the Japanese in the Philippines; Tito's partisans were often mounted during operations in Yugoslavia; and at the end of the war an entire Russian Corps of horse-riding Cossacks that fought for the Nazis surrendered en-mass to the British in Austria. In fact, Russia still uses mounted Cossack units to patrol its borders today.

In post-war occupied West Germany, the US Army's constabulary units set up to police the country used several horse-mounted units.

Today operational cavalry units can be found in several Latin American countries, Germany, Switzerland, Italy, Austria, Britain and the US.

Horseman can quite easily, and with great effect, replace a slow-moving foot soldier in modern warfare in many occasions. Horses are not limited to roads and trails and provide superior mobility to wheeled or tracked vehicles. Horses can be used to track bands of insurgents over any terrain and for long distances as, unlike that foot soldier, they do not easily tire. When used in a rapid reaction force they can quickly encircle and trap insurgents.

A horse can provide surprise, being quieter than a vehicle or helicopter. As several police forces are rediscovering, it can use its sense of scent to find of humans. Once thought to be the role of military scenting dogs, horses are used by police to locate missing persons. This same ability can also be used to track down enemy as experience has shown in Africa, where patrol horses have detected and alerted their riders to the presence of an ambush. Being mounted metres in the air means the soldier can see further, allowing them to see subtle variations in colour, shapes and movement. Thus a mounted soldier can devote more attention towards observation, as he is not concerned where his feet are going; the horse is driving.

In a worst-case scenario, mounted patrols have detonated mines or booby traps, with the horse absorbing the impact, leaving the soldier unharmed.

It is another myth that mounted units are only used in terrain that is unsuitable for anything else. Sometimes they are used simply because they are the right tools for the job.

In World War I, military vehicles were still new and semi-unreliable, so horses were still reliable forms of transport compared to trucks and needed little upkeep or specialisation.

When Hitler rebuilt the German army in the 1930s, most cavalry units were mechanised. However, many units retained horse-mounted squadrons within their formations. One such formation, the Leichte Division that took part in both the invasion of Poland and France, still consisted of mounted riflemen.

Operations on the Eastern Front soon showed horsemen were still needed. Mounted patrols were far more effective in the snow and sticky mud. Many German commanders unofficially reformed their own mounted units and eventually the army officially formed several mounted regiments while the SS formed at least three cavalry divisions. The latter was used primarily in anti-partisan duties, but more mounted units were being formed by the army right up to the war's end.

There are few places in the world a horse cannot operate except for extreme altitude and dense jungle. And in comparison to mechanical equipment and logistical requirements, they are quite cheap to maintain. Essentially horses require a bridle, saddle and in some cases shoes.

The War Horse

A war horse is often thought to be a huge cavalry charger or a smart officer's mount. Historically, however, its role has been much more varied. At the outbreak of World War I, thousands of horses were needed to serve alongside soldiers, whether being ridden or transporting supplies. Therefore the army needed different types for a variety of roles. Riding horses ranged from 14 to 16 hands (one hand is 10.16 centimetres) and used by cavalry units. Draught horses—usually 16 hands or more—switched from pulling buses to hauling heavy artillery guns or supply wagons. Small but strong multipurpose horse and ponies (a pony is fewer than 14 hands) carried shells, ammunition, the wounded or any other task that required horse power.

Military horses may also be divided into classes, such as cavalry horses, mounted infantry horses and gun horses. The best horses by tradition go to the cavalry; they are strong to support an average soldier's weight plus nearly the same weight in equipment. Given this load, a good cavalry horse is expected to conduct scout work, ride up and down hills all day and conduct hurried retreats or charges at full gallop under fire. To aid the horse's rest, the cavalry man is frequently seen walking next to them at every opportunity.

The mounted infantry horse does not require to be the same type of animal as the mounted soldier uses his horse as a mode of transport to the battle, then dismounts to fight. These horses in many armies were sturdier cob types around 15 hands high.

Finally there are two types of gun horse used by the army, Field battery horses and horse artillery. Both types are strong, the former are heavier and usually draught animals, whereas the horse artillery are slightly lighter to be able to deploy the artillery around the battlefield at speed. Such breeds as Cleveland bays still used today by Royal Horse Artillery. A battery of six light guns needed 110 such horses to take to the field.

There are always exceptions to these roles of course, in Australia the Waler was the mount of the Light horseman and arguably the finest mount an army could go to war on. Many British and Indian army cavalry regiments are now stocked with the Waler. It is a strong hardy animal ideally suited for the harsh desert conditions the ANZACs found themselves in World War I.

If a horse was not quit up to a cavalry mount standard it was used in a support role in this case to carry the unit's machine gun. Photograph courtesy of TriColby

This breed thrived as a cavalry mount between 1800 and 1950s. During World War II, 360 Walers were purchased by the Texas National Guard's 112th Cavalry. The regiment initially patrolled the Mexican border until posted to New Caledonia in 1942 under General Alexander Patch. Patch thought about using these Walers to patrol the dense jungle, but after the heavy rains and mud took their toll on the health of the horses the general decided to get rid of them. They were then posted to Burma and used by Chinese forces who mistreated them. Luckily, by 1944, the Walers rejoined the US army being assigned to Merrill's Marauders as pack animals. The 112th sister cavalry Regiment the 124th was the last US Cavalry unit to give up their horses when troops were themselves posted to Burma. Today you can see the Waler on ANZAC day parades proudly ridden by re-enactors.

Another breed worth singling out is the Welsh pony; which have been used by the British army in a number of roles in the past. They have been used to pull artillery and equipment through terrain where motorised vehicles could not go and used in the mounted infantry role. They were considered by the British army to be used in the 1982 Falklands War and again used in 2007 by UN patrols in the

Balkans. Again in 2011 UK Territorial units conducted experiments with these and Dartmoor ponies as pack and riding animals on exercises in Devon and Cornwall, where the terrain prevented vehicles to traverse.

A breed called cavalry blacks is used on Royal and State occasions in the UK. They belong to the House Hold Cavalry Mounted Regiment—HCMR—and are predominantly black Irish draught horses around 16 hands. These horses are purchased at around four years of age and take around 10 months to train before being deemed ready to go on a parade. One of these training requirements is to have an ability to stand still for long periods of time when on guard duty. Like police horses, they must be impervious to traffic noise and be tolerant of the general public. The cavalry blacks do not have a combat role anymore ,but the troopers themselves, if needed, could adapt to riding horses on any overseas mission that required.

Another breed of horse that has a long history of military service and can still be seen today in a combative role is the Haflinger, used by Austria, Switzerland and Germany. They are ideally suited to Alpine terrain, where they have been used for hundreds of years. The 6th Infantry Brigade of the Austrian army maintains around 70 horses today. They have been breed to ride yet solid enough for draught work in the mountainous regions of its native land. Haflingers are always chestnut in colour with flaxen mane and tail and stand between 13.2 and 15 hands.

Some of the other traditional breeds include Arabians; Andalusia's a highly valued Spain war horse; Mongolian ponies; the Exmoor pony, which is the oldest and purist British native breed; the Friesian, a breed used by the Romans; and many classed as Warm Bloods from Europe.

The type of horse used depended on the work to be performed, the weight they needed to carry or pull and the distance travelled. In ancient times Knights would travel to the battle on a small riding pony, such as a palfrey or ambler as it also known which had a gentle looping gate. They would then switch to a heavier mount for the battle that could carry the knight's armoured weight. The most common war horse in this period was called the Destrier, similar to a modern hunter.

Today many Special Forces in places such as Afghanistan use locally bred horses that are inherently suited to the environment they are patrolling. In this part of the world they are called Lokai, an eastern type with heavy Tersk influence. The Tersk, which is basically an Arab-based breed, was introduced into the area to improve local blood lines. The Lokai stands around 15.2 hands and by tradition only stallions are used in war.

Chapter 7: Modern Mounted Operations ⭐»

Today soldiers do not use horses to charge at enemy positions rather they are a mode of transport to go where no vehicle can operate. Photograph courtesy of by Staff Sgt. Robert M. Storm

There are several modern examples of horses are being effectively used today to conduct counter-insurgency operations.

Overall World War II was hardly a low-intensity conflict, but some areas were fought behind the front lines. The most notable in regard to the use of the horse was the German army's counterinsurgency operations in Yugoslavia from 1943-45. A major element of the German Army, which was involved against the Partisans was the Cossack

Division which was recruited from a variety of sources included prisoners of war, Russian emigrants living in Germany or Axis territories and anti-communist volunteers known as "White Russians". They were often commanded by German officers and their role was to patrol and guard lines of communication and deep penetration raids against partisan strongholds. They were often very successful, nearly capturing Partisan leader Tito himself on one raid after destroying his headquarters, capturing documents and many troops. After the war the unit's commanding officer in 1950 provided information to the Americans on how vital horses are in counterinsurgency operations. It stated: "Mounted troops are able to observe mines and booby traps. Horses sensed the presence of the enemy and provided warning. Horse can fight delaying actions and hit and run missions. They are ideal to envelopment operations."

In the 1950s, the Cold War was in full swing and many US generals wanted to r-earm the Germans to fight the Soviets. Many knew then that to win a war in Europe you will need to use the horse. These lessons have not been lost even in today's military doctrine and they were still fresh in the minds of the Portuguese military in the 1960s.

The Portuguese colonies on the African mainland consisted of Guinea Bissau in West Africa and Mozambique and Angola in the south. Between 1961 and 1974, the Portuguese conducted a counter- insurgency war of their own using just under 200,000 troops in the process. In Angola several communist-backed groups were fighting for independence and the Portuguese 1st Cavalry Group, consisting of three company-sized squadrons, provided long-range patrolling and flank security for conventional troops. The country had poor roads and difficult terrain, but the mounted troops were still able to patrol up to 50 kilometrees a day. One squadron was recorded to have patrolled 500 kilometres between 8 August and 1 September in 1971.

Africa continued to be a hot spot for uprisings and the next country to fall was Rhodesia in 1980. Rhodesian officers had been attached to the Portuguese cavalry and took back many lessons in the use of mounted troops. Two main reasons horses where still viable then was both Angola and Rhodesia are free of tsetse fly and a good military truck cost more than a platoon of horsemen. So in 1974 a small mounted unit was raised; No 1 Mounted Infantry, better known as the Grey Scouts. Their role became virtually that of traditional cavalry, reconnaissance, intelligence-gathering domination of areas, locating enemy units and delaying them until stronger forces arrived.

The unit grew overtime, starting with 12 horses in 1974. Its main role became a pack-transport unit to resupply forces trapped by that year's particularly heavy rains and flooding. Very quickly they rose to 400 men and by 1979 had become a 1,000-strong unit with veterinary staff divided into two regular squadrons. The Grey Scouts were very successful in their role of cross-border raids, patrol missions and counterinsurgency operations. They usually conducted these in eight-man teams on patrols of up to seven days. If they contacted the enemy ,they would either fight themselves, usually dismounted on foot, or call in for paratroops.

Eight men could cover the same area of ground a 500-man infantry battalion could. The horses were always in action until put out to pasture at the end of the conflict when the new country of Zimbabwe was established. Such was their reputation, the Zimbabwe National army later recreated the 1st Mounted Infantry with black soldiers from the original Greys. The new unit even used the Greys' old badge, Alas after a few years it was disbanded. Many of the white officers who were vital for training the mounts had left to start a similar unit up in South Africa.

Australian Light Horse re-enactor travelling around Europe with his horse and mule for charity.

US Security Police Squadron-Present ⭐⟫

USAF Security Police 2012 grooming his horse prior to patrol. Photograph courtesy of by Staff Sgt. Robert M. Storm

The Air Force with horse? Mounted Air Force go back quite a way in the US. Horses used to patrol bases at Panama, as they were the right tool for the job. The 23rd Security Forces at Howard Air Base in that country used five mounted patrolmen to cover the immense area of the base and its surrounds. Other Air Force Security units that operated horses were Clark Base in the Philippines and the Air Force Academy. They have even had a resurgence in the past few years with another Air Force horse patrol opening and an increase in mounted staff at another.

One of the busiest bases is Vandenberg, which has utilised horse for many years to conduct patrols, search and rescue operations and surveillance. When required, they are also used in crowd control and general law enforcement. Vandenberg's horse patrols commenced in 1996 to employ a more environmentally friendly mode of transport for the 30th security force's game wardens. The horses are the key for patrolling this nearly 1,000-hectare base, where terrain ranges from remote sandy beaches to rugged hills chocked by dense scrub.

In the USA, the horses at Vandenberg were recognised for their outstanding work recently. Upon their retirement the two of them were awarded meritorious service medal. The two 540-kilogram retirees, one called Judg,e a 27-year-old quarter horse who has served for 20 years at both Howard and Vandenberg bases, and Willie, an 18-year-old Arab with 14 years' active-duty service, will be put out to pasture at an equine sanctuary. However that's not the end of their working days, the pair will be helping disabled children learn to ride and balance.

When their citations were read out to a crowd at Vandenberg base people were amazed at what they had achieved. Judge had patrolled 19,000 kilometres of jungle whilst in Panama, and had captured more than 100 trespassers. At Vandenberg Willie and Judge had located drug hides worth more than $3 million, had prevented numerous demonstrations at the missile base, catching four infiltrators. One of their last assignments was to train US Navy SEAL teams in horsemanship and mounted tactics prior to their deployment to Afghanistan.

Other Countries

With the withdrawal of the Portuguese in 1974 from Angola, other neighboring south western African states began campaigns against South Africa with relative impunity. The South African Defence Force organized a separate arm to wage war against the counterinsurgency. This force was called SWATFS which stood for the South West African Territory Force it consisted of several specialist units including a tracker dog and horse mounted wing. Horses were used over rough terrain or when noise discipline was needed. It was noted that the more complex the operation the more the mounted unit was employed. A usual tactic was for standard infantry in armoured cars would conduct sweeps proceeded by mounted troops some 1000 meters behind.

Today's South African Defence Forces mounted unit operates out of Potchefstroom equine centre, which is also responsible for breeding and training. The mounted arm is organized into platoons of 64 men with 42 horses. Of the 64 men 34 are riders the remainder being support staff such as farrier, veterinary staff and stable hands. As such this allows the unit to operate independently and can be attached to other units when and where they are needed.

Other countries that maintain horse mounted units include China, where vast spaces still require cavalry to border patrol long borders. These units are more akin to police or border patrol units, but come under central army control. In Tibet, the army employs two battalions of cavalry and a number of separate frontier guard companies who are issued with horses and mules for pack transportation. The Chinese have not forgotten that everyone that has ever successfully invaded their homeland has done so on the back of a horse. The latest was Japan only 70 years ago. Every Japanese Division had a horse-mounted company on its strength and proved very successful in China's remote rural areas. This same landscape is still much the same today. Anyone invading there in the future will no doubt have to turn to equine transport.

The 61st Cavalry Regiment of the Indian Army is one of the few remaining non-mechanised mounted units in the world today, unlike the British Household Cavalry or the 11th Cavalry Regiment of the Moscow Military District which tend to be only ceremonial.

The Russians still maintain horse transport companies in the Far East region within the 34th Brigade. The pack horses are used while undertaking missions in hard-to-reach areas and as the only unit of its kind has an elite status. Only those members who can work under adverse conditions and have the passion to work with horses are selected.

We have taken much from the war horse over thousands of years. After World War I the public demanded that they be well treated and rewarded for their contributions in winning the war, yet it took another generation to build monuments such as London's war animal memorial to finally recognise their deeds. Recent films such as *War Horse* has again sparked interest.

Chapter 8:
Marine Mammals ⭐≫

Having worked in the zoological industry myself over a number of years, I am aware how controversial a dolphin working in the military will look to most people. The very idea of using such an intelligent animal to do man's dirty work evokes great emotion to some. However, all may not be what it seems. Marine mammals are used to save lives in military and are treated better by the military than in most marine parks that I have seen. They are a highly valued asset and, unlike tourist-orientated marine shows, money is not the guiding factor in their employment.

There has been great pressure from various lobby groups in the USA to ban the use of dolphins in any form. One example of behavioural enrichment which by the uninformed onlooker might seem like crass entertainment is training sea lions out of the water to perform what look like various tricks. But before this training commenced, if a vet required to check on the health of a captive sea lion they had to drain the pool, separate now-stressed animals from one another, tranquillise the animal in question just to take a sample of blood, weigh them or check their teeth. However by training the sea lion by food reward to jump out of the water onto a blue mat, for example, you can eventually place a set of scale underneath it and thus weigh the animals. The same process can train it to open its mouth or raise its flipper on command, so eventually you can inspect its teeth or take blood. It looks like party tricks, but has a scientific and health basis.

In the late 1980s Richard O'Barry, Flipper's original trainer was active in the training and release program for former military dolphins. One of the first dolphins used by the US Navy was Tuffy in 1965. He was used to drop off supplies and messages to underwater habitats manned by naval staff. He was found to be the most effective method of dropping these items off consistently at 70 metres' depth.

Today many more marine mammals are used in similar ways to either rescue man directly from underwater entrapments or to collect materials from the ocean that could not be done by man or would greatly endanger man's life if they tried. The US Navy Marine Mammal Program centred in San Diego is part of the Alliance of World Marine Parks and Aquariums. This international organisation is committed to the care and conservation of marine mammals and the Navy exceeds all the standards set down for animal care, husbandry, conservation and education. All naval handlers conduct an accredited course and all teams have an experienced civilian marine mammal trainer attached to them. These civilians also deploy on operations around the world to ensure the highest of animal care is maintained.

A persistent myth that hangs around the use of dolphins in the military is they are used to attack enemy divers or ships. Apart from it being simply not true, a dolphin could not possible know the difference between the hull of an enemy ship or your own or identify the difference between a US diver and say a Russian one this type of warfare would be haphazard at best. However, the Soviets maintained they taught their dolphins to distinguish between friendly and enemy propeller and engine sounds. US naval animals are trained to detect all mines or swimmers in the area of concern and report back to their handlers who then decide upon an appropriate response.

One example of the value of marine mammals was on operations during Enduring Freedom, when sea lions were deployed to Bahrain. The sea lions were tasked to locate and retrieve maritime-listening devices that had been deployed during the war. Many hundreds of these expensive and secret devices littered the ocean floor. Using traditional scuba divers would have taken many months to locate and retrieve them all. This is mainly due to a human's limitation of both depth and the amount of dives per day a naval diver can do. The sea lion has no limits frequently diving to 150 metres and using their inherent smell, underwater vision and hearing—most torpedoes having a pinger that gives out a constant tone—to locate the devices.

The recovery team consists of an inflatable boat, two sailors and a sea lion. The devices, once located, are retrieved by what is really a very basic method. The sea lion has in its mouth a bite plate, with a rope attached to it. When it locates the device the two arms at each end of the bite plate clamp around the missile once the sea lion releases pressure from its mouth—like scissors but in reverse mode. The sea lion gives the rope a few tugs to make sure it is secure then swims back to the boat grew who simple pull the device up on the rope. Not a single human sailor gets wet during the process and the sea lion gets a reward—in this case a fish.

The US Navy has used marine mammals since the mid-1960s, today they use two species the bottlenose dolphin and the Californian Sea Lion. Both are known for their intelligence, trainability and adaptability. All the functions the sea lions and dolphins do are natural behaviors, they are both intelligent creatures and it has been my impression from seeing them do the work, that they enjoy playing the game. The US Navy also has researched the use of two beluga whales, one called Morgan was used under Arctic conditions to dive to 500 metres and recovered lost torpedoes.

U.S. Army
Veterinary Staff ⭐»

The advantage with dolphins have is their advanced sonar capability which allows them to locate objects in dark and dirty water. Photograph courtesy of US Navy Marine Mammal Program

The marine mammal program is supported by the US Army Veterinary Corps. The Navy takes great pride in providing its marine mammals with the finest veterinary care. A veterinarian and technicians are on call around the clock seven days a week. Due to the speculation and criticism of the program ,the Navy has become very transparent in this area. These open policies have resulted in the Navy's postgraduate animal care and training internships. This is voluntary hands-on work for civilian students, exposing undergraduates to various aspects of marine mammal training and care. Participants also conduct research projects at one of the country's top marine management facilities.

The US Navy and private sector have not given up on trying to replace animals for underwater operations. Blue Fin 9 is a project is based on underwater sonar that duplicates the dolphins' sonar and can detect hidden mines on the seabed floor. It is great in theory but has limitations. Apart from costing millions, it takes a team of humans to operate and program it. It cannot autonomously think for itself and only moves on a preprogrammed route, unlike a marine mammal that can think for itself. One thing all unmanned vehicles have in common whether in the ocean, land or air is they are extensions to man, whereas a dolphin or sea lion can replace man underwater.

The USN have found sea lions are cheaper to operate than other marine mammals as transport costs and requirements are easier. Sea lions respond better to changing conditions. Dolphins also have to seek an object via sonar whie a sea lion can be trained to seek objects via commands using all its scenes.

Surviving the Cold War ⭐》》

Having been employed for while at a marine park and having several friends that have worked over the years at places such as Seaworld, where love and passion for dolphins was paramount, this next story is abhorrent to animal trainers. In the former USSR, dolphins were used until 1984 to guard the Sevastopol Naval base in the Crimea. Unlike the US Navy's commitment to ethical treatment and training, ex-Russian naval staff have stated their dolphins were used to attack divers. This would be achieved by the dolphin being trained to swim into a person underwater at speed in the format of a game and would be rewarded by food for doing so. It is unlikely, since we believe animals do not understand they knew they were killing people by doing so. A harness could also be strapped onto the dolphin with an underwater harpoon or pistol to effect a better kill. There was also a nose cone device that contained a needle with a carbion dioxide cartridge, when rammed into the diver the compressed air would cause an agonising bends-related death. It has also been reported that dolphins were trained to carry out kamikaze-type missions. Explosives, this time strapped onto the harness, would initiate when in contact with an enemy submarine—similar in concept to the Russians in World War II who used dogs to blow up tanks. It is believed at one time that the Soviet had 2,000 dolphins trained for these missions.

At the end of the Cold War many assets were sold off and during the Navy's break up, it was the Ukrainian Navy that inherited the dolphin division. Again, according to a former trainer, the unit once had 100 animals but now have four due to financial reasons. The Russian Navy closed its marine mammal program in the 1990s, however reports in 2000 stated in what must be one of the most bizarre military hardware sell-offs, 27 dolphins were sold to Iran.

A former Russian naval dolphin trainer Boris Zhurid stated to the BBC press that he was forced to sell dolphins, beluga whales, walruses and sea lions to the Iranian navy after he had run out of money to care and feed them. The Iranians are in a constant struggle to control the narrow Straits of Hormuz, through which much of the world's oil is exported. It is here Zhurid claims the dolphines will be stationed. Apart from employing them in the similar work of locating missing mines and torpedoes like the US Navy dolphins, the Iranians might retain their more sinister attack role.

During the late 1980s the US Navy operated five dolphins in the Persian Gulf area to protect US ships in harbour, allegedly the Iranian Navy then machine gunned any dolphin they saw, fearing that they were American spies or were laying mines.

Then US Secretary of the Navy, Gordon R. England, visits Explosive Ordnance Disposal Mobile Unit Three and their Mark Six swimmer defence dolphins. The dolphins were deployed to the Persian Gulf to provide operational force protection capabilities for naval ships, piers and other high-value assets as part of the global war on terrorism. The dolphins are trained to detect, locate and mark threat swimmers and divers attempting to commit terrorist attacks. US Navy photo by Christopher Mobley.

Chapter 9: War Dogs ⭐》》

The use of war dogs is not new. Well before the Romans, Egyptians, Greeks and Babylonians, fierce fighting dogs were used in battle. In Egypt, murals dating back to 400 BC commemorate the fighting spirit of dogs in combat. English soldiers in the 1600s used dogs not only in war, but to track down highwaymen who fled justice. In the US, similar hounds were used to track down slaves and prisoners of war during the Civil War.

From these beginnings, military dog training and employment has been continually refined to produce a highly sophisticated and versatile extension to a soldier's own senses. Among the dog's abilities that far exceed man is their sense of smell. Dogs are reported to have many thousand times the number of receptors in their noses compared to humans ,with a much larger proportion of the brain devoted to scent. Dogs rely on their sense of smell much the same way humans rely on their sight.

Despite the increasing complexity of military operations, the value of dogs has not declined. In fact, there are more dogs used by the British, Australian and American forces today than in World War II.

Today, military dogs enhance and complement the capabilities of their detachments, often saving vital time and money. They enable one handler with one dog to be a force multiplier, having both a physical and psychological over others. There is a saying in law enforcement which would be echoed in the military, too; one dog is worth 50 men.

Dogs are ideal for tasks such as tracking, detecting explosives, locating casualties and attack work. Even the most complex machines employed by the military today are unable to duplicate the operational effectiveness of a military dog.In the right environment, a dog can detect an enemy ambush a kilometre away using smell, sight and hearing.

What other piece of kit can detect an intruder on a military base in the pitch black of night, be commanded to chase after him using only a vocal command, scale a fence, jump a ditch, swim across a creek and either on command again attack him outright or bale him up via barking to indicate his presence?

Dogs are invaluable to ground troops in any environment, from jungle warfare operations, as demonstrated by US and Australian tracker dogs in Vietnam and more recently again by Australian troops in East Timor; to the sands and urban areas of the Middle East, patrolling in extreme heat to detecting roadside bombs. They have been successfully employed in Kenya, Cyprus, Hong Kong, Kosovo, Northern Ireland, Iraq and Afghanistan since World War II.

Little wonder that, with the escalation of international terrorism, there has been an increase in the use of dogs in the services. The US military has about 2,800 active duty dogs deployed around the world, with roughly, at the time of writing, 700 in Afghanistan and Iraq.

On common role military dogs have been employed in is guarding bases during peace and war. Their ability to cover and detect intruders over large areas is a cost-efficient way of protecting vital assets. As a young new dog handler, I spent many a year pounding up and down the tarmac of an airfield, just me and my dog guarding multi-million dollars facilities and aircraft for a basic airman's wage.

Over the centuries, dogs have had many other roles. In the past they have done everything from catching rats in the trenches to being deliberately exposed to gun fire to identify enemy positions. However, today's dogs are given more humane tasks, where their specialist skills can do the most good. For example, tracker dogs are used to detect ambushes and to pursue the enemy once located. Many special forces units have, as part of their selection training, escape-and-evasion lectures which include many hours of both theory and practical sessions on how to avoid dogs. One of my tasks as a dog handler was to instruct the SAS on this very subject.

Mine detection dogs—MDD—were first used in World War II to help quickly clear the way for frontal assaults. This role has not changed much over the 70 years since then. More recently MDD have been used in Bosnia and Herzegovina and have proved to be an important asset due to the speed in which they can render an area safe. Many United Nations mine-clearing agencies are using dogs in Cambodia and other war-torn regions, where the dreaded, timeless explosives still take the lives of innocents decades after being laid.

Casualty-detection dogs and similar search-and-rescue—SAR—dogs have been finding wounded soldiers on the battlefields for decades. In World War I they

RAAF Explosive Detection dog teams operate at vehicle check points to ensure the safety of bases. Photograph courtesy of Dave Skeels.

would venture out alone in no-man's land carrying medical supplies and water. If they found a wounded soldier they would run back to fetch a medic, but were taught to ignore a dead soldier. Likewise SAR dogs are today used by the Austrian military for the same role and to aid civilian authorities during natural disasters such as avalanches. Similarly, the Israeli military uses dogs to look for victims in collapsed buildings after suicide bombings.

Military police use dogs to detect narcotics. Drugs, of course, do effect a soldier's ability to think and fight, so drug-detection dogs are an important military asset. They also can detect hidden drug labs and storage areas, thus putting drug lords out of business that otherwise might use profits to fund terrorism.

Whether the object is murder, intimidation or government disruption, the bomb is a favourite weapon of the weak and terrorists. One of the most effective countermeasures is the Explosive Detection Dog—EDD. Beyond doubt the EDD is a commander's most valuable force multiplier on current Coalition operations today. There are more EDDs in the military today that at any other time in history and the numbers will only increase in the future. The British Army has more than 400 such dogs in this role in operational zones throughout the world, with five killed in Afghanistan and Iraq since 2001.

Perhaps one of the most controversial uses of dogs—due to the recent bad press at Abu Ghraib Prison in Iraq—is to guard prisoners of war. Likewise, the guard dog's image had already suffered from World War II images of German dogs attacking victims in concentration camps. So why use them still in this role? It comes down to firstly using them professionally and when this is done one dog can guard hundreds if not thousands of PoWs at a time. This frees up military assets that would over wise to tied up guarding them. During the first Gulf War, I saw a single British Royal Air Force dog and handler guard 800 PoWs. They are effective in this way because they can intimidate people; especially from some cultures where the dog is feared or reviled. Military police can clear a riot or demonstration of many hundreds using a couple of dogs.

Unlike ancient times, both war dog and soldier are valued more by society and the armies they serve, so greater protection is afforded to both. This comes in the way of body armour for both man and beast. Dogs can also wear rubber boots and goggles for protection. Communications and video systems are attached to dogs harness so the handler can see and command his dog in the heat of battle and allow him to recall him if necessary to safety.

Throughout history the bond between dog and man during combat is the stuff legends are made of. The relationship represents everything from father and child, best friend and protector, mate and confidant. There are things I have told my dog in a foxhole I wouldn't tell another soul. From the enemy's prospective, the first thing they will see is fur and teeth smashing down on his arm, to me I see a loyal eager to please, hardworking partner that can locate people, firearms and explosives. When all these attributes are put into one package then the military dog's value is apparent.

In 2012 a British army sniffer dog died after his handler was shot dead while on patrol in Helmand Province. Lance Corporal Tasker of the Royal Army Veterinary Corps, attached to the 1st Battalion Irish Guards, and his dog Theo were inseparable. Theo held the record for the number of finds of homemade explosives and weapons in Afghanistan. They were out on one such search patrol when they were caught in crossfire. Tasker died from his injuries while Theo lacy by his side. The dog was not injured but died of a fatal heart attack when the patrol returned back to base Bastion. They were buried together.

A quote from the Australian War Dog Association states: "During Afghanistan the Australian Defence Force (ADF) have lost nine dogs in combat-related operations. However, those dogs and their comrades have saved many hundreds of young

Some members of 2CER with dogs recently returned from overseas operations, not all teams made it back alive. Photograph courtesy of ADFTWDA

diggers lives by their detection of roadside explosive devices over the last 12 years."

A similar comment was made about Australian and US tracker dogs in Vietnam, where records state dog teams saved an estimated 10,000 lives in that war.

I am a War Dog

High on a hill overlooking the sea,
Stands a statue to honour and glorify me.
Me and my mates that have all gone before,
To help and protect the men of the war.

I am a war dog, I receive no pay,
With my keen, sharp senses, I show the way.
Many of us come from far and around,
Some from death row, some from the pound.

I am a member of the canine pack,
Trained for combat and life on the track.
I serve overseas in those far off lands,
Me and my master working hand in hand.

I lift my head and look across the land,
Beside my master, I await his command.
Together we watch as we wait in the night,
If the enemy comes, we are ready to fight.

In the plantations of Nui Dat I do camp,
The smell print of the VC, to track, as I tramp.
"Seek 'em out boy!" my master does call,
Through the vines of the jungle, together we crawl.

I remember the day we were trapped underground,
With military wildfire exploding all around.
My master and I packin' death through the fight,
Comforting each other till the guns went quiet.

My master's tour of duty has come to an end,
Vietnam he will leave, I will lose a good friend.
No longer will we trudge through the jungles of war,
The canine, the digger, the memory will endure.

Now the years have passed and I patiently wait,
For God to receive me through His celestial gate.
Where I'll roam in comfort for evermore,
He'll keep me safe from the ravages of war.

Reproduced by kind permission Santina Lizzio

Seamus Doherty and EDD Mick at American Army Vetenary HQ, Mogadishu.
Photograph courtesy of Seamus Doherty

Chapter 6:
Pack Animals ⭐≫

Mules are used today in many coutries to haul heavy loads and artillery.
Photograph courtesy of by Staff Sgt. Robert M. Storm

An animal with a pack can travel anywhere a soldier on foot can. The British Army started using pack ponies, mules and donkeys in large numbers in the Napoleonic wars of 1803-15. This continued during the 19th century alongside the use of other animals such as camels in Asia, Africa and the Middle East. On the North-West Frontier of India, the nimble-footed mules of the Indian and British East Indian Company army carried huge loads in mountainous terrain. This included special artillery guns that could be taken apart and transported by teams of eight mules. On the Western Front during World War I, pack animals were often used to carry supplies to the frontline where roads were inaccessible. The same forces were still using them in World War II in the jungles of Burma.

Generally animals in military service will be expected to carry a greater payload and over greater distances in more challenging circumstances than in civilian life. Alongside this demand there is an increase in the amount of food and water required. This is not a sentimental animal welfare issue, but one of key military importance. Without attention to proper nourishment, their performance will deteriorate, rapidly affecting tactical operations. It was not uncommon on long-distance patrols to have half the mules carrying supplies for the operation and the other half carrying food for the mules.

Apart from the more well-known beasts of burden mentioned above, many other ungulates—hoofed animals—were used on military operations to haul or carry stores.

Oxen

Around the world oxen were used as pack or draught animals, usually from within the local area of operations. The British army, for example, used them in wars up to World War II from Abyssinia to India. They are not as reliable as an equine and not suited to frontline work, where they are flighty. They are well known with a light load to be able to traverse difficult terrain. On flat going, they can travel more than 3 km/h with a load of 70 kilograms. Oxen are good swimmers and cope with strong currents and deep water. They can survive on lower-quality food that other ungulates.

Ancient breeds of cattle and oxen were used as draught animals both in military and agricultural circles. When used in the draught role, a pair will be yoked together. Traditionally a team of 16 oxen were used to pull a supply wagon. During the Zulu War of 1879, oxen frequently covered 25-30 kilometres a day. Oxen seem to be particularly sensitive to only working in an environment they find familiar and were known to die quite readily in cold and wet weather.

In India, oxen traditionally have been used to pull wagons as opposed to being pack animals. The method here was to attach them to a wagon with yoke and pole. By World War I, mechanical transport was gradually being introduced in the Indian Army. It nevertheless continued to rely heavily on thousands of locally sourced oxen for many years. The US Special Forces experimented with using oxen in 1997. There were several reasons for this, apart from being familiar with their use when operating overseas; one being they could forage off the land, were cheap to buy, and if you run out of food, they taste okay. They are less subject to diseases than horses and are harder to steal.

Water Buffalo

Water buffalo were mainly used in the Indian sub-continent for draught work. They are slow, powerful animals able to draw heavy loads considerable distances. Their management is much like that for oxen, except they are even better in boggy or marshy environments. Chindit forces during World War II in Burma used water buffalo during deep penetration missions in dense jungle. They probably still remain the best form of pack transport in a monsoon season in this part of the world. In more recent times the Vietnamese army used them to tow artillery along the Ho Chi Min Trail. Today, Brazil's army is experimenting using them in operations in the Amazon. This area has 27 military bases with few roads and fuel is scarce, with many rivers in the area are too shallow to navigate. The Amazon border stretches more than 11,000 kilometres, three times the size of the US border with Mexico, and the army is tasked to control cocaine and diamond smugglers. The army considered mules as pack animals, but due to disease and their requirement for special food, it was decided to use the buffalo.

Reindeer

As with the water buffalo, it makes sense to use local animals that are already suited to the terrain and climate of the area you intend to operate in. The use of reindeer in warfare might seem almost comical, but not only Santa had the idea to pull supplies by sleigh. In Finland during the Winter War between Germany and the USSR, more than 100,000 reindeer were used by the military for raiding patrols, supplying transport and carting wounded to field hospitals. Supplies were either towed in a sledge or carried in packs on their backs. Finnish soldiers would be towed behind them on skies. They were even used as a light horse in more open ground. Later in the war, the Germans invaded the Arctic circle and Lapland and used reindeer, citing them as the only animal capable of operating in deep snow.

Even up to 1960, the British army still listed reindeer as their preferred transport in the Arctic region.

This Photograph courtesy of of Finnish Army sledge teams is timeless and even though taken in WWII, they still used them on exercises in 2013.

Yaks

China's People's Liberation Army used yaks during the invasion of Tibet and still utilise them as light haulage there and in other mountainous border areas. So too do their opposite numbers in the Pakistan/Chinese border area. Both the US 10th Mountain Division and Britain's Royal Marine Commandos underwent a yak-handling course to retain these skills in case needed as late as 2011 after a climbing training exercise in the Himalayas.

Llamas

The Israeli Defence Force, US and Chilean armies have used llamas in limited military applications and reports show promise for their future expanded use. Attributes such as a quiet demeanor, controlled reactions, self-sustenance on sparse vegetation, ease of training, resistance to dehydration and athleticism all combined to make the llama a viable option as a pack animal in combat operations.

Llamas have been exposed to fire fights and covert night operations whilst transporting weapons systems on extended backcountry manoeuvres with special forces recently and the results were very promising. The limitations seem to be their overall load carrying capability is low compared to a donkey or mule. A llama when full grown is around 1.7 metres tall, weighing around 130-200 kilograms but can only carry around 25 per cent of its body weight. Another limitation is availability to a lot of European armies, as they are natives to South America. On the positive side, llamas are naturally adapt to mountainous terrain and to high altitudes, they are very effective foragers, requiring only 5-10 per cent intake of a horse or mule doing the same work.

Llamas although native to South America are used by several International Armies as pack animals. Photograph courtesy of TriColby.

Dogs as pack animals ⭐»

Dogs are used in a variety of roles from guard dogs to rescue dogs.
Photograph courtesy of USAF

Dogs can carry more weight kilo for kilo than a horse and have been used as pack and sledge animals for thousands of years all over the world. During World War I, the Allies made extensive use of dogs to tow machine guns in and around the narrow trench systems. During World War II, the German 6th SS Mountain Division Nord dog section comprised of sled dogs known as Ziehhunden. There were 30 men assigned to this section, known as Hunderfuhrers or dog drivers. Their job included hauling supplies to the frontlines and evacuating the wounded. There is no official estimate of their success, but one soldier's diary stated in 1943 he evacuated 340 wounded troops from the front alone. Dogs also pulled in tandem a canoe-shaped device called a pulka and a similar Finnish sled called a akja in snow. In summer, wheels could be fitted to use them in different conditions.

Today, dogs can still find a place hauling supplies and wounded soldiers during modern wars. In Greenland, dogs are used by the Danish Navy stationed at Arhus on Operation Sirus, which maintains Danish sovereignty and conducts military surveillance in the island's north and nort west. The operation has been running for 55 years and its dog sled teams have clocked up more than 750,000 kilometres of patrols. The Greenlandic dogs themselves are impressive beasts; they are large—around 50 kilograms—and the average Sirus dog will run 25,000 kilometres during its working life. The dogs are descended from animals the Inuit people brought there 5,000 years ago. They sleep outside in all weather and have thick coats and furry feet to cope with the extreme temperature. For the soldiers they are a living alarm, giving advanced notice if a polar bear approaches. On the other climatic extreme, dogs used by the Colombian army in the narcotic wars there are used as pack dogs during jungle patrols, weaving in and out the dense undergrowth that otherwise would need paths cut if they were to use mules.

Horses as pack animals ★》》

Pack animals are used by all major modern armed forces today, here US Army mule carries part of an 81mm mortar and a Russian pack horse is loaded up for winter operations in Siberia. Photograph courtesy of Military Horses.com

A horse's huge power and strength make it a valuable resource for haulage. They can efficiently transport many times their own weight for long distances when harnessed to a wagon. Depending on the load, they can work in teams of two, four or six horses. They have being pulling loads and harnessed as war chariots in this way even before man rode them in war. There is ancient evidence from the Sumerian Empire of equines pulling heavy four-wheeled war chariots, while the Egyptians solely used two-horsed lightweight chariots rather than ride them. In the modern era, horses have pulled everything from agricultural implements to the local milk delivery van and in war they simply exchanged those loads for guns or supply wagons.

Logistics was often seen by many military men as beneath them, and so in the British and many other armies around the world, between the 17th and 19th centuries commissariat departments were formed to carry an army's supplies by wagon or pack. These were essential, as large armies during these periods travelled thousands of kilometres on campaign. Wellington's army for example used large numbers of locally purchased wagon teams during his Spanish and Portuguese war.

During World War I, soldiers found themselves entrenched in static positions and depended on supplies being brought up to the front. These supplies consisted of everything imaginable from ammunition, food and equipment, to letters from home. Equally one of the most important tasks for the wagons was to transport the wounded and sick back to field hospitals. These light ambulances drawn by four horses were invented by Surgeon W. Williams.

Where roads were either badly damaged by shells or flooded by rain and quicksand-like mud, wagon teams turned to pack animals. Pack horse usually carried artillery shells three on each side up to the front, many suffered horrible fates. Some drowned in the mud, while many were deliberately targeted by enemy artillery and killed as they approached the front. Horses continued to be used as pack animals in World War II and Korea. One example was a horse called Reckless. I had first learnt about Reckless from Robin Hutton who has been a major campaigner to have Reckless immortalised in a bronze statue.

Reckless is an American animal hero, she worked for the US Marine Corps who honoured and promoted her for her deeds. Reckless joined the marines to carry 75-millimetre ammunition to the front lines for the recoilless rifle platoon of the 5th Marines. She was locally recruited by Lt Eric Pedersen who paid $250 of his own money for her from a young boy called Kim Huk Moon. The only reason Kim sold her was to buy his sister an artificial leg after a land mine accident. As tragic this was for the Kim family, it was the marine's gain.

Marines loved Reckless not just because she did all the heavy work, but she had a personality. If she was hungry and a marine left his food unattended, Reckless would eat it. And her appetite was legendary; her favourite meal was scrambled eggs and pancakes followed by her morning cup of coffee. But anything was on the menu including Hershey bars, Coca-Cola and even blankets.

During the savage battle of Outpost Vegas in March 1953, where some 28 tonnes of bombs rained down upon the hill complex, Reckless was there. She carried ammunition up the steep 45-degree mountain trails under fire. And the appearance of this little white faced mare would enhance morale. On one day alone, she made 52 trips from the ammunition point to the front lines, 95 per cent of the time by herself. She carried 386 rounds of ammunition which is almost five tonnes. She walked more than 70 kilometres through rice paddies and up hills usually under fire. She would then carry wounded soldiers down to safety and despite being twice wounded, did not stop. Not so surprising not only was this little horse respected but it earned her a promotion to Sergeant. So beloved was she that when incoming artillery fire came into base camp, marines would take off their own flak jackets and put then over her.

Her military decorations include two Purple Hearts, Good Conduct Medal, Presidential Citation with Star, National Defence Service Medal, Korea Service Medal, UN Service Medal, Naval Unit Commendation and the Republic of Korea Presidential Citation, all of which she worn on her red and gold blanket on parades.

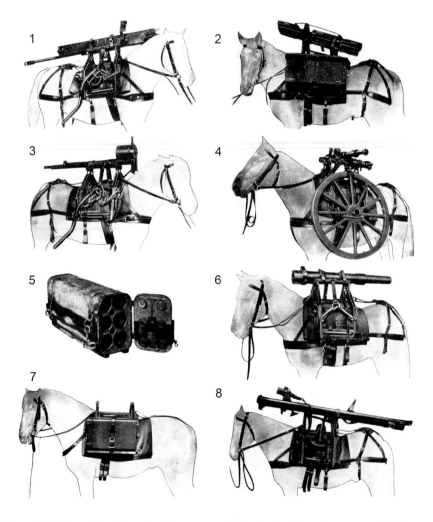

Type 41 Mountain Gun Packhorses as illustrated in a Japanese Military Handbook, 1944.

Chapter 11:

Special Forces ✪≫

US Special Forces still learn skills of their predecessors that may one day be needed again. Photograph courtesy of by Staff Sgt. Robert M. Storm

Special operations forces typically make use of the most sophisticated military and intelligence gathering gear available. All this has to be transported and sometimes a no-tech solution is the best option. When special forces find themselves involved in operations in rural and remote environments, a pack animal such as a donkey or mule is an ideal option. Apart from carrying equipment, horses have also been used to carry the soldiers. One example is the Special Forces mission in Afghanistan in November 2001, just two months after the attacks on the World Trade Center. The highly sophisticated team found Afghanistan anything but modern and the best way to get around was by horse. With the help of local Northern Alliance forces, the adaptable US team mounted up and rode side by side with their allies. According to their unnamed captain:

> The members of the Special Forces A team arrived very early in the Enduring Freedom campaign, with no knowledge they would be riding horse into combat. None had riding experience but undaunted they spent the next 30 days in the saddle fighting with our Northern Alliance partners in the rugged, isolated mountains of northern Afghanistan, relentlessly pursing Taliban forces. Joined by other rebel groups this unique force numbered almost 2,000 mounted soldiers when this particular campaign ended with the liberation of the northern city, Mazar-e-Sharif, it looked like something out of Lawrence of Arabia.

This swashbuckling story is an exciting and inspiring tale but has deeper implications for warfare in the 21st century; be ready for anything, including methods you might think obsolete. The success of such operations led to the US military to establish horse and pack animal training again as we have seen held at both the US Marine Corps Special Mountain Warfare School and at the Army Special Warfare Centre in Fort Bragg.

Interestingly, part of a soldier's Special Forces qualification requirements, along with parachute, scuba diver, mountaineer, medic, engineer; he must also be "horse-qualified". These courses are frequently run by civilian mounted police organisations. One, however, is run by retired Master Sergeant Larry Jones who became an Special Forces legend over 22 years of service and is considered an expert on military animal operations.

The events in Afghanistan have shown that locally recruited horses are the best. They are not used in a cavalry role, but rather to transport the Special Forces soldiers to the fight; the motto being four hooves outrun two feet.

These modern Special Forces teams were not the first such elite groups to use horses and other equines in modern times. In World War II, ANZAC soldiers filled the ranks of the Long Range Desert Group—LRDG. Apart from this unit's famous desert exploits, they operated behind enemy lines in the mountainous snow of the Italian Alps and amongst the hills and forests of Lebanon. They went to Greece, Albania and Yugoslavia, during which time the LRDG made extensive use of mules for logistics and rode donkeys or mules like dragoons. Today, like the Americans, the ANZAC troops are in the forefront of using equines in Afghanistan. The Australian SAS operating out of Bagram had four donkeys purchased from locals, which proved to be invaluable for carrying gear up steep terrain otherwise impassable by vehicle. The members who looked after them gave them all names and no doubt were honoured to carry on the ANZAC tradition most famously depicted in Gallipoli legend.

During the early stages of World War II, Orde Wingate created the Gideon Force named after the biblical figure, from troops of a Sudanese British-led battalion and Abyssinian soldiers from the Ethiopian army. All up, around 2,000 men and 18,000 camels were used for transport. The camel came under Laurens Van der Post who went on to be a famous author. The force set off for Abyssinia in December 1940 to attack Italian forces there. The horse-mounted Sudanese troops made it in five days, while the camel troops took two weeks.

Major General Wingate went on to form another organisation called the Chindits which was the largest Allied Special forces unit during World War II. The Chindits operated deep behind Japanese lines in the Burmese jungle for months at a time, relying on air drops for supplies. Wingate remarked he could not have fought the campaign without the mule. The mules carried everything from heavy weapons, ammunition, radios and medical supplies. Some of the airdrops to the Chindits not only included fodder for the animals but included mules themselves being paradropped in. In the same theatre, mules were used with great effect by Merrill's

These mules and troops in 2012 are doing the same job
their ancestors did in World War I. Photograph courtesy of AWAMO

Marauders an American outfit. The Chinese army was supplied 20,000 mules to battle the Japanese.

The US Marines have a long history of using mules, including between 1927 and 1933 while suppressing an insurgency against the Nicaraguan government by a group calling themselves Sandinistas, after their leader Augusto Sandino. The Marine expeditionary forces consisted of the 5th and 11th Marines Regiments within them was the 52nd Mounted Company. Initially mounted on mules, they switched to horse in the rugged mountainous jungle of the Nueva Segovia region. These horses were really ponies; the average being 13.1 hands. They carried a rider and/or cargo of around 100 kilograms. Being local mounts they fed off the land on 45-day patrols. Not once did the 52nd fail to complete a patrol in this rugged country, even during times when men had to dismount and cut a path through the jungle for the ponies.

The Commander of the 52nd noted how the ponies helped prevent marine casualties in several ways, firstly they could detect an ambush. The Sandinistas usually aimed at the horses not the men, when laying down, the horses provided cover, travelling on them allowed the marines to be more observant of their surrounds, the marines were also not as tired as those who had to walk.

Special forces have been quick to use war dogs' special talents, too. When US President Barack Obama went to Fort Campbell in 2011 to visit the commando team that killed Osama bin Laden, not all the members had two legs. In fact the

US Delta Force Para dog.

only SEAL team member that has ever been identified and name released to the public was Cairo, a 30-kilogram Belgian malinois.

Dogs used by the SEALs are highly trained, highly skilled and highly motivated. The dogs carry out a wide range of specialised duties for their teams. Among other things, they can detect explosive materials and locate hidden humans.

The dogs are twice as fast as the fittest SEAL member, so anyone trying to escape is not likely to be outrun by Cairo. When SEAL Team 6 hit bin Laden's Pakistan compound, Cairo's feet would have been four of the first on the ground. The dogs, equipped with video cameras, also enter certain danger zones first, allowing their handlers to see what ahead before humans follow. SEAL dogs are trained parachutists, jumping either in tandem with the handler or solo if the jump is into water.

SEALs are famous for being underwater experts and as such form part of the US Navy's elite Special Clearance Team 1, currently headed by a Force Marine Recon Captain. The team consists of about seven dolphins and a mix of Special Forces personnel from the SEALs, to British and Australian SAS members on exchange. During a search, a dolphin will locate a mine and return to the support vessel. A diver then can either recover the mine or send the dolphin back with a small charge, that it places next to the mine. Once safely away it can be detonated.

The US Navy has found the biological sonar of dolphins, called echolocation makes them uniquely effective in locating mines. Echolocation basically allows the dolphin to construct a mental image of the object by bouncing a series of clicks it produces off an objects and receives them back (US Navy's Marine Mammal Program).

Nearly every Special Forces mission can benefit from the inclusion of dogs in their team, they are a proven, low technology combat capable asset.

United Kingdom Royal Marine Commandos.
Photograph courtesy of UK Ministry of Defence

Chapter 12:
Ceremonial ★>>>

Photograph courtesy of TriColby

Our modern view of military animals often turns us to parades and pageants where we view spectacular-looking horses riding ahead of royalty. Public duties and state ceremonials form part of the fabric of a nation and offer a powerful symbol of military heritage, whilst enhancing the standing country before an international audience.

One such traditional mounted unit still used on ceremonial occasions today is the British House Hold Cavalry stationed at Knightsbridge, London, which maintains a proud tradition since 1660. Even though it has a ceremonial role, every man on parade is first and foremost a fighting soldier fully trained in armoured warfare. Their horse training is held over 12 weeks, where soldiers learn everything they need to know about riding and taking care of a horse.

Another is the King's Troop, Royal Horse Artillery. All its soldiers are superb riders trained to drive teams of six horses that pull a World War I-era 13-pounder gun. As far as ceremonial duties the Troop fire Royal salutes on the Queen's Birthday or state events and provide a funeral gun carriage on special occasions.

It was initially named the King's Troop in 1947 by George VI following the mechanisation of the last horse-drawn artillery unit, as he wanted to preserve this tradition. He named it after his title, but on Queen Elizabeth's accession she declared the name would remain the same to honour her father. So esteemed is this unit that when on parade it takes precedence over all other regiments. The unit's 111 horses are based in St John's Wood, London. Even though primarily a ceremonial unit, King's Troop riders deploy to Afghanistan as drivers of ammunition carriers to artillery units.

Most of these type of ceremonial units all have farriers, vets and support staff already in their infrastructure and many of their officers come from equestrian backgrounds. It is quite possible that a unit such as this deployed on active service might find it prudent to have a platoon-sized mounted unit complimenting its armoured vehicles. This did happen to members of the Royal Scots Dragoon Guards during a KFOR—Kosovo Force—deployment in 2001, when they obtained local horses to patrol areas their vehicles could not. Captain Tom Bateman who commanded the mounted patrols in the Slivovo region stated: "We have met an incredible reaction from the locals, who are not used to seeing KFOR patrolling in the hills from the backs of horses."

I know myself from policing, if you position a mounted officer in the middle of an intersection within an hour he will be surrounded by people patting the horse and talking to him. This is often a great source of information or intelligence gathering. Yet if you park a police car, within five minutes the street is empty. No-one ever pats a police car. Maybe the military could get a message out of this type of patrolling on UN peacekeeping operations?

Even ceremonial animals face danger by terrorist groups such as the IRA. In 1982, a car bomb exploded as the Blues and Royals made their way to the Changing of the Guard ceremony. Four Troopers and seven horses were killed. Sefton, a Household Cavalry horse, was badly injured in the blast and became a national hero after recovering from his wounds, which included a severed jugular, damaged left eye and 34 additional wounds over his body. Sefton returned to his duties and, with the courage befitting a cavalry horse, made no fuss when on parade he walked past where had been so badly injured. Another horse who also survived the blast was Yeti. Badly traumatised, he returned to service until 1986 when he retired to a rest home in Buckinghamshire. He died years later at the age of 36.

Australia has a long and proud history of mounted troops both in its colonial wars and during the Egyptian deserts of World War I. Sadly today Australia does not have a full-time ceremonial unit in the armed forces. However it does have many Light Horse re-enactment troops who volunteer their time to parade at official events to keep the history alive.

At war's end on 11 November, 1918, the 11th LH Regiment was in camp at Tripoli, north of Damascus. The troopers and their horses had become as one, and each hoped he would return to Australia with his faithful horse. It was not to be. Some of the best horses were to be retained for the Imperial service. The rest were to be destroyed. The 11th had to remain overseas to help police the area and did not get back home till August 1919, after four-and-a-half years abroad.

After World War I, the 11th Light Horse Regiment, became a militia unit between the wars. In World War II, it was reborn along with its horses as a regular part of the army. However the 11th Light Horse Regiment was "dehorsed" in 1942 and became mobile and mechanised unit.

The current 11th Light Horse Troop is a re-enactment group formed in early 2003. They are not regular soldiers in the Australian Army although some of their members have served in the ADF.

Their members come from all walks of life and are dedicated to upholding the proud traditions and equipment of the Light Horse. Their members purchase and maintain their own equipment and receive no regular government funding.

One of these army units is the 1st Cavalry Horse Detachment—full-time solders of which more than a dozen members have recently returned from deployments in Baghdad, Iraq. When back in the US, they maintain 18 horses and nine mules for historic preservation, community service, public demonstrations and ceremonial duties. At their home in Fort Hood the 1st Cavalry routinely take fellow soldiers, from retiring troopers to generals, for a ride.

In 1967 the US Marines Corps Mounted Colour Guard was formed at their logistics base in Barstow. They ride five palomino horses initially purchased back in1968 by a retired Marine Lieutenant Colonel. Today they ride palomino

In any circumstances, it is a sad day when a soldier gives his life for his country: however, some are given the honour of being escorted to rest via carriage. The US Army maintains such a sunit, and sadly it is used far too often. Photograph courtesy of www.army.mil

mustangs caught wild from the Bureau of Land Management adoption program. The colour party travels all over the US, representing the corps at parades, rodeos and numerous other events.

In several Scandinavian countries, ceremonial horse are also used in emergent rescue operations and during arctic warfare exercises. The Life Guards in Stockholm is the only regiment in Sweden that has horses and an equestrian training centre. They are used in the same way the British Household Cavalry operate, on royal family occasions, static mounted guards and other state ceremonial occasions. Like their British counterparts, their secondary role is armoured reconnaissance, but they have also been used in the mounted role to test the viability of their mounted use in modern warfare. Interestingly during these trials, their warm blood parade horses remained in barracks and soldiers were mounted on locally hired native ponies.

In Finland, the cavalry Regiment—Uudenmaa Dragoons—has a ceremonial function but maintains skills for guerilla operations on horseback in the high Arctic. Soldiers are skilled in using horses and pack mounts. They have proved under these conditions and terrain they are still viable over more modern means of transport.

They exchange their parade horses for small fast Icelandic ponies in the field.

Lord's Strathconas Horse—Royal Canadians—is a fully mechanised tank unit using Coyote Light Armoured Vehicles—LAVs—and Leopard tanks. The unit has had members continually serve in Afghanistan on rotations since 2002 as part of task force Kandahar. In 1977, it reintroduced a ceremonial horse-mounted troop to maintain the traditions and history of the regiment. There are currently 25 riding members who volunteer for two years on horseback. Daily functions include training and cavalry drills. In 2000, to commemorate the centenary of its original foundation, a mounted detachment of 18 members were invited to London where in full ceremonial dress they mounted the Queen's Life Guard at Horse Arch for a week. They remain the only overseas unit to ever have the honour to mount the sovereign's mounted guard.

These mounted skills, like their Scandinavian counterparts, could be used in Afghanistan by Canadian troops if they ever need to conduct mounted operations in-situ. In their own backyard, this unit would be capable of conducting patrol

U.S. Marine ceremonial unit- this same unit can also use horses if need be to patrol mountainous or desert terrain. Photograph courtesy of US Department of the Interior, Bureau of Land Management

operations in the country's tundra wilderness. In both locations, rather than their parade horses, the US icon the mustang with its big hooves and dense bone structure is readily available and ideal.

Many military police throughout the world use animals in law enforcement. Whether riding a horse to chase down a deserter on the battlefield in the 1700s to guarding prisoners of war with guard dogs in Bosnia, military police will continue to use animals as a force multiplier. I have mentioned them under the ceremonial chapter as they are frequently seen in this role protecting royalty or VIPs. Military police horses were used, for example, when Lady Diana married Prince Charles. He was escorted by the Household Cavalry, but she was escorted by a troop of Mounted Military Police as she was a commoner.

Heavy horses although not as famous as their Cavalry relations, do however the bulk of all military horsepower work.
Photograph courtesy of RAASC web site.

Chapter 13:
Mascots

Mascots come in different types; the official mascot and the odd mate you pick up on your tour of duty. Photograph courtesy of TriColby

Military mascots have been of great morale value to soldiers from the trenches of World War I to animals adopted by coalition forces in Afghanistan today.

Some are owned by a regiment and are part of their official history. These animals have a regimental number and rank and are paid for by the defence force.

An example of one of the earliest recorded types belonged to the Royal Welsh Fusiliers during the 1775 American war of Independence; it was present at Bunker Hill. This mascot goat has had many successors in the regiment down to the present day. Some of the same official types are the British Parachute Regiments pony, the New York National Guards Wolfhounds or the US Marine Corps Bulldog to name a few.

There have been all types of animals that have served the colours in this official capacity, and nearly all have a tradition behind their choice. The Royal Fusiliers have an Indian blackbuck associated with that regiment's extensive history in the subcontinent. Some have a connection to their unit's origin such as the Newfoundland mascot of the Canadian Rifle Regiment.

Official mascots are entitled to the services of the army's vet service, as well as quartering and meals at public expense. Some mascots' costs are borne directly by the regiment itself not the Defence Department. One such animal was Major, a white bull terrier in World War II serving with New Zealand troops in the Middle East. Major served until his death in 1944 and was buried with full military honours.

Some mascots are as famous as their regiments, some for good reasons some not so. An Australian army Shetland pony Sergeant Septimus Quartus or "Seppy" the official mascot of the First Battalion Royal Australian Regiment (1RAR) was honourably discharged recently after 17 years' service, even though he has been charged with insubordination one year. He has taken chucks out of soldiers during marches, has kicked his superiors and visiting dignitaries and hates anyone who wears black. Seppy is a long line of regimental ponies in this unit, his great-great grandfather had a penchant for the ladies and often went AWOL. The Australian army has released the official records from all four Shetland pony mascots and it reads like an episode from the comedy TV series *MASH*.

Operation Baghdad Pups

Another type of mascot, usually a dogs, are the unofficial animals many soldiers have adopted in the battle zone. Some US troops in Iraq and Afghanistan befriend local animals as a way to help cope with war's emotional strain.

This is far from new and soldiers have had pets they pick up on the way since man first went to war. Most war ships have a cat onboard and soldiers in World War II in Burma would often adopt a monkey.

The problem then until recently was many a loving bond had to be broken and the animals left behind due to quarantine restrictions or military orders forbidding such pets.

Today the Operation Baghdad Pups program provides veterinary care and coordinates complicated logistics and transportation requirements in order to reunite these beloved pets with their service men and women back home in the US. Another group called the Guardians of Rescue which for several years have collected donations to bring dogs back from combat zones work with a private Kabul-based organisation to send dogs back to the US. It costs about US$4,000 for every dog rescued from a war zone.

Opposite: Smoky the world's first PTSD dog has a monument in the USA and his place of birth in Brisbane, Australia. Photograph courtesy of Bill Wynne

Chapter 14:
Therapy Animals ⭐》》

SMOKY
YORKIE DOODLE DANDY
AND
DOGS OF ALL WARS

The soldiers and their horses from the 3rd US Infantry Regiment at Arlington also known as the Old Guard, are one of America's oldest active-duty units; formed in 1795. Its main role today is laying national greats and service members to rest with dignity, respect and honour at Arlington National Cemetery. They also participate in important ceremonies throughout the country.

Since 2006 they have taken on another mission, providing physical and psychological therapy for wounded troops, particularly amputees.

Many soldiers returning from Afghanistan and Iraq have suffered these types of injuries from roadside bombs. When available between ceremonial obligations, the horses are used to help soldiers learn to walk again. Horses have been used by medical experts since World War I to help strengthen limbs and balance. This therapeutic riding also promotes emotional healing. Horses and people walk using the same circular motion in their hips, and riding on the back of a horse can help a person feel and recall that movement.

It's not only horses that are helping servicemen, man's best friend is also helping to rehabilitate physically and mentally wounded service personnel after the horrors of war.

Post-Traumatic Stress Disorder—PTSD—has been around since the first wars. Often misdiagnosed or misunderstood, dogs have been used since World War II to help service members rehabilitate with love, affection and an ability to be nonjudgmental. In the US, President Bush in 2001 signed a law authorising the Veterans Administrations Department to underwrite programs such as Canines for Combat Veterans to assist with the rehabilitation of soldiers. Apart from veterans suffering from PTSD, many too have physical injuries which they will need help with all their lives. Service dogs are a 24/7 companion that can retrieve and carry objects, open doors, importantly they can help be a bridge to society from combat duty to civilian life.

So successful have dogs been to help rehabilitate service personnel military, occupational therapists have been assigned to the 113th Combat Stress Control Medical Detachment in Kandahar, were dogs have been introduced into the war zone to replicate the benefits troops gain from them on the home front.

Even donkeys can help. A donkey called Smoke was found by US Marines badly malnourished in Tagaddum, Iraq in 2008. The marines nursed the little donkey back to health, built it a pen and stable, eventually making it a mascot. Regulations forbad the marines from keeping a donkey, so a naval psychologist designated Smoke a therapy animal to reduce stress among the marines. Smoke soon made himself comfortable around camp, walking into offices to locate apples or carrots in desk draws the soldiers had hidden for him when they were out on patrol. He would sometimes follow them on long missions.

The marines made a blanket for him with the unit's emblem on one side and the words Kick Ass on the other. The marine's tour was over in 2009 and the relieving army unit did not need a mascot. They tried to get a local to look after him but a year later, marines returning to the area saw him mistreated again and just wandering around behind US troops.

So Marine colonel John Folsom, now retired in Omaha, decided to bring him back to the US. After an 18-month effort of politics and frustration to rescue the former marine mascot from war-torn Iraq, Smoke arrived to take up his new life in Nebraska as a rehabilitation therapy animals for military personnel and their families. Experts say Smoke will be valuable in helping therapists engage children with issues they may about their parents being in a war zone.

Many different animals have given soldiers comfort and aid during the pressures of war. The British soldiers in World War I were renowned for having pets, from kangaroos brought over by Australian troops to injured birds nursed whilst in the trenches. These all had to be left on the enemy's shores when war ended due to bureaucracy. Hopefully in the future these animals will be recognised as a valuable resource to our troops fighting morale and be allowed to come home rather than be thought of as disposable items.

Chapter 15: Animal training establishments ⭐》》

There are several military animal-training facilities throughout the world. They usually include a veterinary corps to provide humane animal care in both peace and war missions. These act in a similar way to civilian organisations such as the RSPCA, but operate in active and post conflict areas by tending to the health care and needs of animals effected by war. They also support developing countries in an advisory role on subjects ranging from animal welfare to agricultural issues. This can be a vital part of any mission. The value of a beast of burden to a tribesman in Afghanistan can be the difference between his family's survival over winter or not. A donkey is their pick-up truck, plough and much more. Any part of any military mission in someone else's country is to win the locals' hearts and minds. A veterinary corps is one of the best ways to do this.

A friend's anecdote perhaps highlights both the importance of animals and their value to military operations and to locals. He was joking with me saying what would he tell his grandchildren when they asked him what he did in the war. His job was to drive around the war zone in a truck filled with goats, the idea being after a coalition unit had been through a village and had aggressive contact with the Taliban, several things usually happened. Firstly the local village head, who naturally had no idea the Taliban were going to shoot at troops from his village, claimed the coalition troops' returning fire had killed several of his livestock.

At first the soldiers would apologise and move on, this often resulted in ill feelings between the locals and troops which could affect everything from them providing sources of intelligence to outright hostility.

So my mate's job was in fact very important to the safety of our servicemen. After any contact he would front up an hour later and give the village compensation in the form of goats and donkeys. So next time you see a special forces member, his life might have been saved by a soldier delivering goats in Afganistan.

The US National Guard's 1/14th Agribusiness Deployment Teams employ citizen soldiers farming experts and come from the agricultural mid-western states such as Missouri, Nebraska, Indiana and Iowa. By teaching local farmers to expand their productions, it is leaving both a positive and economic impact on the locals. Simply put, if they breed more livestock or produce more crops, it promotes a more stable environment for our troops to operate in.

In the past, servicemen tasked to working with animals were recruited from the land, such as farmers, ranchers, game wardens, zookeepers and stockmen. These people were regarded as having the necessary skills to work, look after or train the many animals the military needed.

Today the military training establishments, veterinary corps, dog sections and ceremonial cavalry units look for the same practical, independent, can-do attributes found in rural people. Previous experience with animals may well be an advantage, but the lack of it does not necessarily disqualify an otherwise suitable soldier, and the very same abilities can also be found known as street smarts in youths raised in big cities. The second group of people who find themselves using animals in modern warfare seem to be the special forces such as Marines, SAS, SEALs, Mountain Warfare specialists, or Green Berets.

The Royal Army Veterinary Corps—RAVC—was founded in 1796 in response to public outrage that more army horses were being lost by ignorance and poor health care than on the battlefield. Veterinary officers were first appointed to cavalry regiments, which immediately cut losses. Even more so today, no war that was ever fought or contemplated could have been undertaken without equines. A horse's life in earlier times was cheaply regarded, as they were both easily obtained and commonplace. The RAVC gave these animals care and comfort, today they still provide these basic functions and provide training to animals and handlers alike.

Such a unit in modern warfare is useful after a battle. At the end of the first Gulf War, it was found that many animals in the Kuwait zoo had been shot by Iraqi troops for fun or food, but many were still alive and injured. The zoo had a famous elephant that had been shot and left to die. The RAVC vets were called in and removed 69 bullets and the elephant recovered. They were also able to treat local domestic and agricultural animals that were either injured or stray. The RAVC today employs dog and equine instructors, farriers and specialist saddle makers much as they did 200 years ago.

The US army has a similar organisation to the RAVC, the US Veterinary Service, an integral part of the Army Medical Department. The United States Veterinary Corps—AVC—has been dramatically increased over recent years to fulfil the need of supporting US war animals deployed overseas but to provide support to local animals in those same countries, where they are a large part of wealth, security and status to the local population. In peacetime, the AVC is responsible for providing care to the Military Working Dog—MWD—teams in all four branches, the ceremonial horses, cavalry mounts and animals that work for the Homeland Security organisations. They also look after the pets of servicemen deployed overseas at no charge. This is another important moral aspect to their work which eases the worries of their own servicemen.

Animal training, however, is done by a mix of military and civilian organisations. The Air Force predominately trains all military working dogs, however both the

US Marines and Army engineers train explosive and mine-detection dogs. Both these types are also outscoured to private contractors on occasions, depending on the level of urgency. Likewise, the US Marines train pack mules for themselves and the army, but civilian pack animal courses are also undertaken, mainly run by ex-special forces experts such as retired Master Sergeant Larry Jones, the man who literally wrote the book on today's military use of pack transport. The US Navy SEALs were recently trained to ride by the Dallas Mounted Police Department.

Petty Officer 2nd Class Blake Soller, a Military Working Dog (MWD) handler, pets the head of his MWD Rico, at the War Dog Cemetery located on Naval Base Guam. Twenty-five Marine War Dogs gave their lives liberating Guam in 1944. They served as sentries, messengers, scouts. They explored caves, detected mines and booby traps. US Navy photo by John F. Looney

Chapter 16:
Use of paramilitary units to patrol borders ⭐》》

US Marines on horseback can be used to aid civil power if required. Photograph courtesy of US Department of the Interior, Bureau of Land Management

Governments spend big to protect national borders. The US, for example, has invested millions in attempting to secure the border with Mexico. But in the age of advanced surveillance, one of the most effective methods of policing such a border may be one of the oldest.

When Congress first established the US Border Patrol in 1924, it was strictly an equine affair. Applicants had to supply their own horse and tack, but the Government would feed the horse. In the very same locations today, in the rocky, desert territory outside El Paso, a sure-footed horse can traverse ground that a four-wheel drive or all-terrain bike cannot.

In Europe, the fall of the Iron Curtain has resulted in virtually open borders, leading to a dramatic increase in illegal crossings. Many countries, due to the enormity of the problem and area of coverage, have turned to the military to assist. But if the military are to help, they will need specialist equipment. For example, a conventional military invasion across the US borders by Canada or Mexico is not very likely, so large mechanised formations of battle tanks will have few applications for homeland defence.

Threats that do exist, however, include terrorists entering a country via land routes at illegal crossing points. This would as applicable in the Austrian Alps as it is over the Mexican border, where both countries are rediscovering the special abilities horses have to protect and patrol the borders.

Horses are also being used in Texas, California and up on the border with Canada in Spokane, Washington. Authorities use wild-caught mustangs, which are obtained from the Bureau of Lands and Forest Department and trained up at various prisons by offenders as part of their rehabilitation. Horses bring an air of authority to explosive situations; their size and speed can be intimidating, but they also have a calming effect on a large groups of detained persons. In these same isolated regions, horses can be used for search and rescue, usually locating the very illegal immigrants or felons whose plans to avoid authorities in the first place have gone wrong.

Their abilities to navigate this type of terrain, cross rivers and climb hills give them not only a capability over most vehicles, but a unique cost-efficient method. It costs less to feed and care for 10 horses a year than to purchase and maintain a single 4X4 off road vehicle. While the vehicle lasts about three years, a horse can be in service for 20.

A lot of borders around the world are remote and many are within large nature reserves or national parks. Many endangered species of animals reside in these same national parks. Unlike vehicles, horses can patrol these areas without ripping up flora and fauna and disturbing animal populations.

Horses are not the only means of transport or use of animals in border protection. China, India and Pakistan all use camels to patrol their remote regions. The dog plays a huge role at the border protection zones from locating smuggled goods to people. The military here have a role to supplement civilian agencies, it would keep both dogs and handlers current and operational skills retained between wars.

It is true that today's helicopters, airplanes and unmanned aeriel vehicles provide a bird's eye view over a last area of the border, but you still need a man on the ground to capture the offenders. The roar of a patrol vehicle's engines or headlights and general lack of stealth often enable persons to escape long before the patrol gets there. A horse or dog patrol that work equally well in day or night has an advantage in stealth and ambush tactics.

Chinese mounted border patrol unit uses fast Mongolian horses.

Chapter 17:
The Future ⭐⟫

Photograph courtesy of Shaun Ward

I see a future for animals in combat in countries where terrain or infrastructure prevents the use of modern conventional modes of transport. There are places in the world you can still not drive a vehicle or where high altitudes limit helicopter use. In environments such as the high tundra wilderness, heavily forested areas, deserts or the Arctic, an animal might still be the best method. Given man's greed for natural resources, these same areas are where the next generation of wars might be fought.

Equines also do not need refuelling or rely on vast logistical support structures, so a mounted infantry unit can be pretty much self-contained. You can go anywhere a man can walk on an equine, by riding to battle and dismounting to fight, you are fresh and you don't have to carry all your stores on your back. Finally, in an emergency, it's a meal on four legs.

Today, in rough terrain, some South American and special forces units from various other countries use formal combat cavalry units for reconnaissance and transportation of themselves, similar to dragoons of the Napoleonic era, where they then dismount to fight. Other professional horsemen today are from ceremonial units or training establishments. Some informal cavalry units around today are usually in the developing world and not recognised by the national army. One such example is the Janjawweed militia seen in Darfur, Sudan, who became infamous for their attacks on unarmed civilian populations. The final group of horsemen today in the military, tend to be ad-hoc formations that although officially sanctioned are temporality raised for a mission or a particular reason then usually disbanded.

There are many high ranking leaders in today's military circles who still believe the sun hasn't set on battlefield a horse-mounted unit couldn't operate in the future. A recent contracted study by the US Amy entitled *The utility of Horse Operations and Pack Animals in Counterinsurgency Operations in the Latin American Environment*, senior officers interviewed all agreed that horse-mounted troops can make significant contributions in low-tech and counterinsurgency operations.

A modern Light Horse force would not only contribute to the security of a nation's borders but would useful should horse-mounted missions be needed in counter guerilla operations. Several of the world's larger armies' approach to small bush wars, counterinsurgency operations or counter actions against terrorist groups tend to be the same, hit them with a big hammer using the latest technology. I see the problem with this approach is not using the appropriate firepower or level of technology against the enemy. Using a special forces unit mounted on local ponies might be all that is needed.

The future of the military dog is without question. It is simply in a league of its

Photograph courtesy of Dave Brown

own. Their advanced scenting capabilities cannot be replicated or improved upon. They are proven to have saved lives on the battlefield and I can see them alongside soldiers for decades to come. Sledge dogs in areas such as the Arctic still possess all the same qualities needed today as they did 200 years ago and will continue to be an asset in that environment.

Bird strikes in both military and civilian airports are a problem causing millions of dollars' worth of damage or hold ups and even the occasional death. Flocks of birds find runways idea nesting sites as man has conveniently removed all the predators. Some airports have even been built over old migration breeding grounds. Military bird of prey that once attacked messenger pigeons could now harmlessly to scare flocks of birds from runways.

Finally with more than 75 per cent of the world being covered or accessed by water and at depths that man cannot venture to, use of marine mammals will remain useful particularly in recovery and rescue roles. In recent years we have seen several deep-sea submarine disasters, one member of the marine mammal program I spoke to said their dolphins were capable of diving and attaching listening devices to both the stricken Russian subs, allowing authorities perhaps to determine were to focus their rescue efforts on. These animals may have also been able to drop off air pipes and attach cables. The problem was no-one asked the unit.

Argintinian Sniper team in transit to hide, even the horses blend into the enviroment. Photograph courtesy of Argentine Military Attaché Canberra

COUNTRIES USING COMBAT ANIMALS TODAY

Norwegian Military Working Dog team are full time soldiers unlike many of the armed forces which is conscript based. Photograph courtesy of Norwegian Embassy.

Israel Defence Forces ⭐》》

Military sources quote the Israel army plans to use llamas for reconnaissance and combat missions in enemy territory in the future. The sources describe them as ideal for special forces missions in Lebanon against Iranian-sponsored Hezbollah terrorists.

Israel sits in an area of the world that has seen animals used in war since before Biblical times. The country's military—the IDF—has found the perfect vehicle for special forces operations: the llama, which was first used in 2011 in the Golan Heights. After extensive tests, this uncomplaining animal was found to easily out-perform donkeys previously used in the same role to conduct low-signature ground missions in enemy territory.

During one such sabotage exercise in Lebanon, llamas carried 50 kilograms of equipment over mountainous terrain. The army plans to train the llamas to carry 100 kilograms, which will greatly ease the burden of troops, who can then concentrate on combat or reconnaissance. Donkeys in the same situation did not perform as well; they made much more noise and required more food and water. A llama would traverse terrain a donkey would not and could be made to sit in a Humvee. The different coat colours make excellent camouflage with white areas being dulled down with paint. On the negative side, you cannot ride a llama and it carries less of a load than a donkey.

The IDF already has spy drones, automated sentry towers and sophisticated sensors to keep watch over its borders. The latest additions to the arsenal is a herd of African eland, each weighing nearly 500 kilograms.

The eland have been stationed in the zones between the high security fences and the southern Lebanese border to clear problematic foliage that distorts the views of soldiers keeping an eye on the Lebanese side. Eland are known for their sharp incisors and appetites. The first eland was brought to Israel as part of a conservation-management program, where local zoos would breed them and return them to Africa were at the time they were endangered. However noticing their lust for the same type of vegetation that grows wild around military bases, the Israeli army over a decade ago as part of a maintenance project.

According to an Israeli National Parks Authority llan Hagai, eland eat huge quantities of weeds and act like bulldozers, clearing areas that also act as fire lanes, preventing forest fires.

There are now around 700 elands eating vegetation at military bases and border areas throughout Israel.Eland of course are not the only four-legged animal used by the IDF. Oketz is an elite combat canine unit and actually precedes the IDF, which was founded in 1939. It was a part of the Haganah, a paramilitary organisation that was the precursor to the Jewish State's current army. Oketz is one of the most highly regarded of the IDF units and few commanders would consider embarking on a mission nowadays without its support. Today just about every terrorist arrest is led by Oketz dog teams. Either a soldier searches a house or a dog does, they minimise collateral damage, harm to civilians and have an immense psychological effect. War dogs can be used in large scale wars the Israeli forces have found themselves in leading platoons of infantry to avoid ambush or detecting booby traps. However, it is during Israel's constant low-intensity operations that they come to the fore.

When I wrote my book *Cry Havoc: The history of the world's war dogs*, I interviewed various military attaches from embassies, including Israel, and found out handlers get assigned a dog of around 18 months of age. It lives and sleeps with him or her for a further 18 months—the length of a basic dog course. They naturally have a strong bond and a handler retains the same dog throughout their career. Dogs are usually German shepherds or Belgium malinois.

The IDF use a human's familiarity with animals in their fight against terrorism in an unusual way. They use fake animals, similar to a child's soft toy. A toy cat might be placed on a roof and people just seem to notice it but pass it by thinking that it's real. The cat in fact hides a surveillance camera or in some cases a weapon system within that can be operated remotely.

Elite Israeli Military Working Dogs, no mission is usually without a team.
Photograph courtesy of C/O OKETZ

Italy ⭐》》

Italy has always used animals extensively due to their northern mountainous border. Mules were used in all modern wars and are still at company strength today in their elite Alpine units. The horse has made a recent comeback, and severak Recon Squadrons of the infntry have been re-equiped with horses over motorbikes.

More than 70 years ago the last Italian cavalry charge in history took place on 23 August 1942 by the Don River. The Italian Savoia Cavalry Regiment, consisting of 600 mounted Italian troopers, charged against 2,000 Soviet soldiers. The Italian cavalry using lances destroyed a pair of Soviet light-armoured vehicles before being forced to withdraw. The Germans made much use of this incident in propaganda but the reality was they were lucky to catch an ill-prepared enemy with their guard down. After this, the Italian army only used horses in small numbers for reconnaissance and as pack animals in their Alpine regiments. However, recently the horse has been reintroduced into the Italian army. Each Italian mounted recon team is made up of four horses and men—one being a signals expert and another a medic. In Italy, there are still parts of the country that cannot be accessed by anything else but foot or hooves. Even in places where an all-terrain vehicle can go, the horse is often faster.

It is not surprising that this progressive country has turned back the clock and is prepared to use old but proven ways. They do after all have a history dating back generations in the use of transporting pack artillery within the Alpini Corps. This unit was formed in 1872 and the oldest such mountain warfare unit in the world. The corps believed one mule was worth three soldiers—just one animal could carry all three parts of a 120mm field mortar and faster than a whole platoon of men. These mules were so revered and such an integral part of an Alpini soldier's life that as part of his initiation into the elite corps a soldier had to eat a cold potatoes warmed by mule urine. You can even be outranked by a mule, as they have their own rank system. It is quite common for a muleteer to be a lower ranked than his charge.

The Alpine Corps' original mission was the same as it is today; to protect Italy's northern mountainous borders. They distinguished themselves during World War I when they fought a three-year campaign in the Alps against Austrian and German Alpine troops in what became known as the War of Snow and Ice. During World War II, the Italian Alpine corps fought alongside the Axis forces principally on the Eastern Front and in the Balkans. The corps today are on operations in the remote mountain villages of Afghanistan.

Troops from the Alpine parachute regiment in Afghanistan initially dismissed the mule and took none with them. It did not take long to realise their mistakes. They use the mules that have been locally purchased to carry medical aid and up to 200 kilograms of rice, blankets and other items to villagers. These type of operations win the hearts and minds of local village elders.

Apart from the Alpini, the Italian Mountain Fusiliers also used donkeys. Each soldier had a donkey to carry their gear and in extreme cases were allowed to eat the donkey.

Apart from horses and mules, the Italian army uses dogs. In Italian history dating back to the Roman Empire, dogs have always accompanied soldiers. The Romans used large attack mastiff type dogs against the Celts and Greeks. By the beginning of World War I, the Italian army used dogs as sentinels, as rescue dogs as light haulage beasts of burden and as messenger dogs. By World War II, the

Italian dogs could be seen guarding prisoners of war and other vital assets such as rail heads and bridges across the country. Today the main breeds of dogs the army use are German shepherds, Belgian maliois and Dobermans.

The Italian air force and army field a number of dog teams protecting domestic military bases and international interests when on operational deployments. They are credited in Afghanistan with reducing infiltrations and detecting any enemy presence. Many Italian war dogs have seen operational action in places such as Kosovo and Iraq. Some have been recognised and received awards for bravery from the Italian President.

USA ★》》

US Army member training in 2011 for mounted operations. Photograph courtesy of Cpl. Nicole A. LaVine

Since the Founding Fathers, the US Military has always used animals in warfare and continues to do so today. War dogs are on the increase, marine mammal are replacements for dangerous deep-diving operations and mules are making a comeback. It is surprising to many, however, to see the cavalry re-emerge. This branch of the services had its heyday on the American frontier in the 1800s and 1900s. By the time World War I broke out, America still had cavalry but not on the scale it once was. The British and Germans still clung onto this traditional arm using more then 100,000 cavalry men in the war. After seeing the horror of the trench war with new machines called tanks and rapid repeating machine guns, the US high command agreed the cavalry charge was over.

When World War II came, horses could still be found in the army; many of them along with mules were used as transport animals. From the USA's entry into the war until VE-day, more than 15,000 horses and mules were processed by the Quartermasters Remount Service. Approximately 11,000 were sent to Italy to support transport problems in rough terrain.

The remount service had long refused to use white horses and mules in combat as they might be targeted more easily. However due to the high demand it was necessary to buy up all the local animals regardless of colour. To the rider or muleteer however it was near suicide to be sent to the front on a white equine, so with some Yankee ingenuity and a mixture of potassium permanganate an animal could be sprayed and discoloured grey for up to 60 days. While in Sicily the 3rd Provisional Reconnaissance troop was organised as a mounted unit and went on to patrol on horse in Italy until 1943. By their mechanisation, they had 143 horses and 349 mules on strength.

In Hawaii, the army and coast guard patrolled the beaches and hills of the islands. On the continental United States army national guardsmen and again the coast guard patrolled the shorelines watching for spies being dropped off by sub.

The Americans claim the last cavalry charge by them was conducted by the 26th cavalry—known as the Philippines scouts—at Luzon in 1942 against Japanese infantry supported by tanks. The 26th climbed on their horses and flung themselves against the enemy guns, it did not succeed and survivors interviewed in 1977 by the *Washington Post* stated the starving army were forced to eat the regiment's noble horse heroes after the battle.

Fighting on horseback is not easy. And thrusting a blade at 50 kilometres an hour into a man-size target is an art form that takes years of practice, so by 1914 the sabre had all but disappeared. The manual had to be rewritten upon its reissue

The Marine Corps' Mounted Color Guard from Marine Corps Logistics Base, Barstow, CA at the Jinx McCain Warrior Riding Program dedication ceremony. Photograph courtesy of Credit USMC Cpl. Damien Gutierrez.

in World War I, it was done so by the man who designed the new model 1913 cavalry sabre: a Leiutenant George Patton.

Patton went on of course to be a great tank general but he never forgot his first love the cavalry. Even his nickname was Sabre George.

The 10th Mountain Division are no strangers to the horse, having established a cavalry reconnaissance unit in World War II. The division was formed at Fort Meade, South Dakota, then sent to camp Hale. Eventually they were disbanded as the high command did not know how to use them properly. The need came for them again in 1944 and a great effort was made to locate and transfer all the original horsemen back to the outfit. This time they would be in Italy, where they began patrolling in the hills above Naples. That spring they were trucked to Florence and met their replacement horses. According to Donald Hubbard, who recalled his experiences in Italy, these horses were a sorry sight. They had been obtained from the Vichy French, Sardinians, Hungarians and Germans and were simply worn out. But to a cavalryman they were a horse. On one operation on 14 April, 1945 in the Po River district the 10th troopers made an attack, rushing ahead so fast that the enemy was unable to establish an effective defence.

Another incident told by Hubbard brings into question if the 26th Cavalry had after all done the last cavalry charge back in 1942. The story goes:

We had advanced within a few kilometres of the Po River when we came upon a small village. The troop was moving in single file with the first platoon in the lead. There were buildings on a side street to our left, suddenly German machine gun fire opened up from a second floor of a stone dwelling. The third platoon commander ordered a pistol charge on the enemy position while the first and second platoons dismounted and prepared to support the assault. What the third platoon lacked in firepower they made up for in courage. Our supporting fire was so successful it suppressed the enemy fire and no horses or men were hurt.

The use of horses in this campaign ended when they reached the Po River at San Benedetto. The part-time cavalry then tied their horses in an orchard of fruit trees, bid them farewell, and crossed the river in boats.

It would not be the sole use of horses in Italy. Once again the horse filled the vital need, passing columns of mud-embedded motor transports. Many leading generals commented in no uncertain terms on the lack of horses and mules in their armies. The horses during the campaign did well considering they lacked the correct diet as the units quartermasters were not used to catering for war horses. Their campaign ended when the unit reached the Po River at San Benedetto. Even without horses, the unit retained its name—the 10th Mountain Cavalry Troop—until 1948.

Many generals sang the animals' praises. General Dwight D. Eisenhower, in a report in August 1943 stated horse cavalry units should have been used in Tunisia if they had been available. General George S. Patton said that in almost every conceivable theatre of operations, situations arise where the presence of horse cavalry is vital. "In North Africa had we possessed an American cavalry Division with pack artillery in Tunisia and Sicily, not a German would have escaped," he said.

General O.N. Bradley stated that it was not just his but many general officers' opinions that, had he possessed a cavalry division that could race through mountainous country and get behind and hold the enemy, victory would have been less expensive in terms of casualties.

Even in Vietnam, US troops were asking for horses during mountainous operations for the same valid reasons. Some US and locally indigenous tribesmen used local ponies to ride or transport heavy fire power up jungle pathways.

The US has used and will no doubt continue to use the noble equine in war, and although one of the world's biggest users of war dogs, it was well behind the ball game in their use at the start. Granted dogs were used by the founding fathers against Native Americans and the British, however they were usually a local idea or an individual's and war dogs did not appear on the army's official records until the Second Seminole War, when 33 Cuban bloodhounds were brought at a cost of several thousand dollars to track down escaping Native Americans in the swamps of Florida and Louisiana.

During the Spanish-American War in 1898, dogs were used for scouting by Teddy Roosevelt's Rough Riders, when his men were dismounted in the dense Cuban jungle. When the Rough Riders were mounted, the dogs would run ahead of the horses picking up several ambushes that the riders would have surely been caught in. A similar role would be used again by US dogs in Vietnam some 70 years later. In World War I, the US army did not have a war-dog policy and although plans were made, no official dogs were used prior to the war ending. By the time World War II arrived, the army still had no formal military dog unit or plans to recruit and train them.

At the time of Pearl Harbor, the army had decided to employ sled dog teams, sending about 50 to Alaska for training in search and rescue. These teams would later be posted to Greenland and Iceland to rescue any aircrew men that crashed or had to ditch their planes on the way to the UK as part of the lend lease program. Many planes did crash and many aircrew's lives were saved during the war by these teams.

These same teams were requested by General Patton during the Battle of the Bulge to transport supplies to the front as the weather had all but stopped all other forms of transport. Alas they arrived too late to help.

The exception in the US was the Marines. As early as the 1930s, the Marines had been interested in war dogs and had experimented in their use. They had first come across the enemies' sentry dogs in Haiti and other wars in Central America, where dogs staked around guerilla camps in the jungle sounded the alarm at the approaching marines. More than 1,000 marine dogs were trained during World War II. Twenty-nine of these were killed in action, 25 of them occurred on Guam, where there is a beautiful memorial statue of a Doberman honouring them by artist Susan Bahary. Six dogs were recognised for heroism on Bougainville with the 2nd and 3rd Marine Raider Battalions.

Eventually the US army did more than catch up in World War II. Initial estimates thought that the army would need 200 dogs, yet about 10,000 dogs were trained for all four services by the time the war ended in 1945.

Like equipment or good ideas in the military, if not needed daily they seem to slip into the shadows. Unlike equipment however you cannot blow the dust off a dog and by the time they were needed again in Korea, the dogs were no more and the expertise in training them in many cases had all slipped away. All the US Army had was the 26th Infantry Scout Platoon. That luckily was enough, the 26th participated in hundreds of combat patrols and became legendary. They served with honour and distinction from June 1951 to June 1953. Platoon members were awarded a total of three silver stars, six bronze stars or valour and thirty five Bronze Stars for meritorious service. After the Korean War, the army dog-training centre remained at Fort Carson until 1957 mainly training air force dogs.

Dogs in Vietnam were used to guard air force bases and other military installations. But one of their most famous roles was patrolling in country for the Viet Cong. The dogs soon learnt to pick up danger signs such as ambushes, booby traps and trip wires. They were also used to find downed pilots, caches of weapons and to track down and hunt enemy patrols. Small highly trained units, usually consisting of five men and a Labrador, were called Combat Tracker Teams or CTT. Their role was to track down the enemy and pursue them. Apart from the tracking skills of the dog the soldiers were trained visual trackers as well. They were usually supported by a much bigger formation a platoon or company but worked alone well ahead to maintain noise discipline and surprise.

In the Cold War, military dogs were again used predominately to guard bases in Europe or the Philippines. They had another resurgence in the 1980s and 1990s under United Nations missions such as Bosnia, Albania, Serbia and Kosovo where dogs where used in patrolling, riot control, arrest of suspects and mine and explosive detection. Since then they have not looked like being unemployed, shortly after these UN missions US dogs were deployed to Operation Desert Shield and Desert Storm where 118 Military dog teams deployed throughout the Gulf region. Today of course, they can be found in Afghanistan saving numerous lives by detecting roadside IEDs and hunting terrorists.

The US may have had a slow start but around 100,000 dogs have served in their armed forces up to today from the snows of Alaska to the jungles of Colombia.

US Marines have used dogs from the 1930s to present day operations in Iraq and Afghanistan. Photograph courtesy of AWAMO

Australia ⭐》》

Farewell to parade to mounted observation unit in Darwin, cut due to costs or backward thinking. Photograph courtesy of ADF

The Waler was the backbone of the Australian Light horse mounted forces. It was especially suited to working in the harsh climate, which suited the Sinai Peninsula and Palestinian deployments. It even proved superior to the native camel as a means of transporting large bodies of troops in this area.

During the Boer War, 16,314 were sent overseas for use by Australian Imperial Forces. In World War I, 121,324 Walers were dispatched overseas to the allied armies in Africa, Europe, India and Palestine. Of these 39,348 served with the First Australian Imperial Forces in the Middle East, while 81,976 were sent to India.

Australia were light horsemen not cavalry. The light horseman combined the characteristics of both cavalry and mounted infantry. This resulted from many factors affecting the Australian Army, least of all the vastness of the country and the size of its relatively small armed forces. Military doctrine also had influenced the formation of the light horse after Australian defence chiefs had studied the recent Franco-Prussian War that had illustrated that massed land armies supported by artillery dominated the modern battlefield.

Since the Australian forces could never adopt a European model, they did things their own way. By the 1890s, the Australian army consisted of small regular forces in each state, supported by large numbers of volunteer militia.

When Australian troops fought in the Boer War, their methodology of conducting war was considered to be the answer for Australia. Volunteer Light Horse Regiments were established all around Australia, supported by rifle clubs that provided semi-trained reinforcements. Should these formations be called upon to defend Australia, the local commander was charged with maintaining resistance in the form of a large-scale guerilla war using commando tactics. This strength-sapping guerilla war was the key deterrent for Australian defence and heavily relied upon fast mobile forces. The mounted infantry were the key.

Light horsemen were like infantry in that they dismounted and fought on foot, using their horses to transport them to the battlefield. This gave them an ability to swiftly engage or retire. They worked in small teams of four men. Three would dismount and fire rifles whilst the other was a horse holder, ensuring the mounts were always on hand ready to charge or withdraw. A Light Horse Regiment contained roughly 600 men, divided into three squadrons—A,B and C.

To discourage the Light Horseman from charging like the European cavalry, they were initially never issued with a sword, although much later on in the war this was changed for some militia and regular troops. However, they used their bayonets if they found a need to do so. One of these occasions was perhaps the last great cavalry action ever seen on a large scale. This took place in Beersheba, a small town situated on the northern edge of the Sinai Desert. Its importance was its wells, as water in any desert battle is vital to victory. If you control the water supply you simply command the area all around.

There have been many books and several movies made about the charge of Beersheba, here is a basic look at the action of 31 October, 1917.

The Light Horsemen were part of a combined British force. The engagement started at 0500 hours and continued all day, with many a gallant action fought that day by Australian, British and New Zealand troops. By 1430 hours the day began to wane and Chauvel knew the town had to be taken before nightfall. The horses had travelled through the desert for three days and most would die if not given water.

Beersheba was held by the Turkish army, commanded and supported by Germans. It consisted of the 27th Division and battalions from the 16th and 24th Divisions. Opposite them 800 Australian Light Horsemen were supported by British Artillery and the New Zealand Mounted Infantry, which also played a key role in the battle.

The British Yeomanry cavalry were there and pleaded to charge but Chauvel choose the Australian 4th and 12th Light Horse. The Australians lined up in full view of Beersheba. Between the town lay heavily enforced trenches and no cover. Every man knew only a wild desperate charge could seize Beersheba, they drew their bayonets and began to trot with a five-metre gap between each horseman. Then suddenly they pressed forward at the gallop, the Turks opened fire with artillery and machine guns, then the Turk riflemen fired.

The Australians dug in their spurs and charged forward, the Turks were so bewildered they failed to adjust their sights and soon their fire was passing harmlessly overhead. The cry rang out: "They're under the guns." The Australians rode to victory, capturing the wells in tack before demolition charges that had been set by the enemy could be set off.

The day of the Light Horseman was not over. They continued in the Middle East to the end of World War I and would be back in the same area during World War II. Although the Light Horse were a mechanised unit by then, they still managed to turn the history books back. On several occasions ad-hoc mounted units were used as they were the best form of transport in that terrain. One mounted unit nick named the "Kelly Gang" rode in several engagements.

Mules and donkeys were also extensively used by Australian troops in Sicily and the Tunisian mountainous regions for supply and evacuation missions.

Even after World War II the Light Horseman under different guises would not go away. In recent times NORFORCE which has a tactical role of reconnaissance, scouting and coastal surveillance across the Kimberley and Northern Territory approaches to Australia brought back the horse.

Like its predecessor established in World War II called the 2/1 North Australian Observation Unit, also known as the Nackeroos, modern-day troopers have found the horse to be the ideal means of transport in this area. Trials lasted up to 2009 before termination but the terrain and problems getting over it have not gone away and the day may return that horses once again patrol this strategically important area.

Many local commanders at low to medium rank level often use their common sense and utilise the right tools for the job, that's the Australian way. For several years the Australian Air Forces Air Defence Guards at Tindal Air Base in the Northern Territory also used horses to patrol the perimeter of the base. This stopped around the late 1990s.

Sarbi and his handler in Afghanistan. Sarbi would latter receive the RSPCAs Purple Cross for bravery. Photograph courtesy of ADFTAWDA

Australian Army engineer sapper and explosive-detection dog in Afghanistan.
Photograph courtesy of Shaun Ward

The Australian army as an entity began using patrol dogs during the Korean War, with further deployments during the Malay Emergency and in Borneo. Dog instruction was conducted to Australian troops by members of the British Army's RAVC.

During Vietnam, Australia trained and supplied two units of tracker dog teams. They became 11 of the most popular diggers to the Australian war effort. They consisted of six Labradors and five lab-cross breeds. They were usually called out to follow up enemy trails or locate suspected enemy hideouts. On many occasions they would catch a ride to the suspected enemy area by helicopter. The dogs loved these flights, finding the cool air blowing in their face a relief from the oppressive tropical heat.

When on the ground, the dog would locate and follow the scent at speed until the enemy was found, when it could stop with noise extended facing the suspected hide or person. The dog and tracker team would then fall back while the rest of the platoon searched or destroyed the enemy.

Today explosive detection dogs rather than tracker dogs are in the forefront of Australia's commitment to the Afghanistan war. Specialist dogs work in the Oruzgan Province locating weapon and ammunition hides as well as detecting roadside bombs.

The Australian military have dogs have been deployed in several areas recently, including the Solomons and East Timor. Units that utilise dogs in Australia are the military police whose dogs have the capacity to track offenders similar to the Vietnam days and conduct a law enforcement roles similar to a civilian police dog. The air force uses the greatest number of dogs, which protect every base. The RAAF also has their own explosive-detection teams to conduct searches at entrance ways or to back up army operations. Engineers have explosive-detection dogs and several are embedded with the special forces. Likewise the SAS and commando regiments have their own canine attack dogs that are currently deployed in Afghanistan.

Switzerland ⭐》》

Switzerland uses horses and mules because they can withstand the freezing temperatures that frequent hit the country. They can carry a rider and up to 100 kilograms of equipment over the deep snow drifts.

A vast amount of Switzerland is mountainous and in winter, blizzards and fog are common, making it impossible to use vehicles or helicopters in high remote areas. In the 1930s the Swiss Army had 60,000 full-time horses and mules, serving in the mountain infantry. Today that number is down to a mere 140 full-time animals. But the Swiss Army has a massive reservist element, where another 9,000 horses and mules can be found. The army pays for the upkeep of the animals and for their defence force is a cost-efficient way of maintaining an arm of service that it does not necessarily need every day but cannot afford to do with out altogether.

The army calls upon the reserves once a year for an exercise to ensure operational effectiveness. This can range from several days to a month.

A Swiss breed called Frieberger is a saddle horse and is used for riding, ceremonial and pack work. The army retains around 350 horses as pack animals and a further 60 as general mounts. They are a reserve unit attached to the infantry delivering light logistics. They have been used in recent disaster situations to reach areas vehicle could not supplying aid and to help recover survivors.

Despite a drop in the number of animals it uses over recent years, the Swiss army has its own veterinary corps—*Kompetenzzentrum*. The veterinary forces not only supply treatment for animals, but incorporate the animal-training staff. This includes Swiss Army horses and military dogs. They have a secondary role to support civilian agencies in response to disasters. Apart from vets and animal training staff include farriers, blacksmiths, saddle makers and support personnel.

As the Swiss Armed Forces is a combination of a large conscript force and a small regular element that constitutes only about five per cent of military personnel, the veterinary and animal trainers are always full-time professionals due to workload. Similarly the army's dog handlers in the military police are also professional soldiers, operating general security, explosive detection and narcotic detection dogs. The reservists operate search-and-rescue dogs and, like their comrades with pack horses, these reservists take their dogs home. In the Swiss system, a soldier, once finished his or her compulsory military training, takes all their equipment, uniform and weapon home. So if you're a dog handler, after your dog handler's course it goes home to. Like the pack horses the army pay for its food.

The handler is responsible throughout the year to maintain the dog at an operational level. They are frequently called on to aid humanitarian missions, locating causalities of natural disasters such as avalanches, flooding or earthquakes. This projects a positive image of service animals to the public and whenever on parades the crowds applaud loudly when the horses and dogs march by.

GERMANY ★》》

The German Army entered World War II with 514,000 horses and, over the course of the war, employed more than 2.75 million horses and mules.

The total loss of horses in the war is estimated at more than 1.5 million. The German Army used the services of 37,000 farriers and 236 companies of veterinarians. Their hospitals treated more than 100,000 horses a day with a remarkable success rate of 75 per cent of sick or injured animals returned to service.

Thanks to the precise bureaucratic record-keeping by German armies, we know that 625,000 horses were assembled for the invasion of the Soviet Union in 1941.

Horse usage grew in numbers as the war went on, regardless of technology gained in many areas. When the German Army came across excellent agricultural stock or cavalry horses from the countries it invaded, it would simply add them to their breeding program or operational units. Even in 1944, one German infantry unit in Normandy required 5,000 horses to function

Of course horses were a primary target for Allied ground attack fighters.

There is a notion that Germany used horses because they had no choice, when in fact it was a tactical decision they made over motorised vehicles which they knew would get bogged down or frozen in Russia.

The Bundeswehr today still maintains pack animals in the Gebirgsjager—mountain troop—Brigade. This unit titled Gebrigtragtierwesen—Mountain Animal Detachment 230—uses both Halflinger horses and mules. They have been stationed in the heart of the Bavarian Alps since the 1980s. They initially were a mountain artillery battalion with several hundred mules. Now the detachment 230 operates 60 mules and 20 horses supporting the mountain troops with logistics. This number is not likely to get any lower as it has avoided other defence spending cuts so far.

The Bundeswehr has recently stated that pack animals are the only real alternative in hauling loads up the side of mountains. The only other option is for troops to carry the burden themselves.

Since World War II, government legislation meant German forces were not allowed overseas. However, their chance came in 2002 when the first mission overseas with the United Nations occurred. The unit sent was pack mules and horses to asset in the border region of Macedonia. Since then, in 2009 German mules from detachment 230 were employed on active operations as part of the peacekeeping force, KFOR in Kosovo and again in 2011 with German Special Operations Forces Command—KSK—in the International Security Assistance Force, Afghanistan. They used Haflinger cross mules to travel silently and unobtrusively with their heavy weapons loads.

German military animals are trained at a central location at Mittenwald. The unit takes care of all animal veterinary needs, training, application and development of pack animal operations. The badge of the veterinary operations and training centre is marked in the upper half by a Haflinger horse head and the background is blue; the colour of supply troops. The number 230 for Mountain Infantry Brigade is shown with colours of Bavaria on the right-hand side. The left part has a green background the colour of the infantry with the Edelweiss—the sign of mountain troops.

Today the army has more than 1,000 operational military working dogs at home and abroad. Military dogs are in Afghanistan and the Balkans assisting with mine detection, explosive detection and helping Afghan polive with general law enforcement in major cities.

Military dogs are highly value in the Bundeswehr and are attached to elite

Germany used reindeer in WWII during the Arctic war against Russia, sometimes animals are the only solution or the best tools for the job.

troop formations such as KSK and Fallschirmjager parachute battalions. Apart from regular tours of duty in Afghanistan, parachute dogs have deployed in 2006 at short notice to the Democratic Republic of Congo as part of EUFOR. Apart from the special forces, the German military police uses dogs on base security and general law enforcement support functions such as riot control, tracking and attack work. They also work with explosive detection. Current military police overseas deployments are in Kosovo and Afghanistan.v

The German Army has always used animals to support its mechanized formations, Germany one of the world's leading high tech armed forces still employ mules for mountain warfare operations. Photograoh courtesy of horsesoldier.wordpress.com

Britain ★»

Britain is famous for their ceremonial use of horses.
Photograph courtesy of C/O RAVC

One of the oldest users of the horse, Britain is rediscovering their advantages alongside its less-glamorous cousin the mule in current areas of conflict. Britain has a history of supporting its troops by using war animals in many roles, such as riding them, using them to carry equipment, to detect ambushes and substances, to deliver messages by land or air and to attack enemy soldiers.

Apart from ceremonial occasions, in the main horses have not be used by the British cavalry for over 70 years, however they have appeared on the battlefield via some individual innovative commanders who required their special talents.

According to the United Kingdom Defence Department's website, there are some 500 horses serving in the British army. The majority of these serve in the Household cavalry and the Kings Troop Royal Horse Artillery, with the remainder in several dragoon regiments and at Sandhurst Military Academy, where they are used for ceremonial events. The remainder are governed by the Royal Army Veterinary Corps—RAVC—which looks after, among many other things, the Queen's horses, pack animals, military working dogs and mascots.

Recent RAVC operations included supply of animals and staff to UN operations in the Balkans, Iraq and Afghanistan.

Due to Britain's long traditions with equines, many regiments would be capable of conducting mounted military operations in low-intensity operations in the developing world or where terrain dictates their tactical use. Today several regiments have been trained to ride Welsh mountain ponies for deployment to the Falkland Islands if required.

To understand England's love with the equine we should go back to World War I, when the British Army only owned eight motor vehicles. The army was therefore entirely dependent on the horse to transportation of men and supplies. Even so, at the beginning of World War I, the army only had 25,000 horses, this was totally inadequate and during the next few weeks 165,000 were recruited from all over the country. Suddenly horses pulling a bus a week before found themselves pulling an ammunition wagon.

Even this was not enough for the war effort and Britain had to import equines from Australia, New Zealand, South Africa, Canada and the US. The horses were between three and 12 years of age and trained as rapidly as possible before being grouped into squadrons and sent to the Western Front. By 1917 Britain alone was using more than 530,000 horses and 230,000 mules. Such was the demand the army, needed 15,000 horses a month to maintain numbers and operational ability. These losses were caused by death injury and sickness and many horses did not even make it to the front. As so many had to be imported, many were lost at sea on the way either from attack from enemy submarines that saw horse and mule transports as a prize target or by death from ship-borne disease. In 1917 more than 94,000 horses were shipped from the US, with more than 3,300 lost at sea.

Finding enough food for the horses and mules was a problem on the Western Front, where the daily ration per horse was 20 pounds—about nine kilograms—of grain. This was about 25 per cent less than a civilian working horse was fed before the war. When even grain was sparse, mules were fed on sawdust cakes. Old soldiers tell stories of seeing horse so hungry they would eat wagon wheels or their stable doors. After the armistice it was thought the war horse had had its day, even in civilian life employment for the noble beasts was dwindling, as in their wartime absence farmers and industry had to improve engines to replace them. The result was by the time the war horse came home, it was no longer needed.

Even so, by the outbreak of World War II, the British Army still had some cavalry units. The last British cavalry charge was in March 1942 when the Burma Frontier Force encountered Japanese infantry. During the war, the odd horse was used by soldiers or commands for a variety of temporary tasks. Military police used them to patrol occupied territory and the signals corps used them to deliver urgent messages to the front if the roads were blocked. On the whole, it was the mules that still found a place in the British army in several World War II theatres.

The British army has never forgotten the mule's importance and the RAVC still maintains several in case needed. Britain also sends troops overseas for muleteer training. The Royal Marines were sent to the USA, north of Yosemite National Park, for mountain training with mules in 2008 prior to deployment to Afghanistan. The mountains here are about three times higher than Britain's Ben Nevis, so the sheer altitude affects even the act of walking. This is where the mules come into their own, carrying all the Royal Marines' heavy equipment.

The British Army also pioneered the use of dogs in warfare, with Lieutenant Colonel Richardson establishing the first war dogs in1916. He used no particular breed at the time, but Airedale were favoured as guard dogs whilst greyhound crosses, collies and lurches were used for running messages between trenches. These came into their own at night or in foggy conditions when it was deemed inappropriate to use messenger pigeons. German shepherds are one of the main breeds used today and indeed were used in World War I. But due to anti-German feeling, they were called Alsatians.

After World War I, it did not take the British peacetime governments long to reduce defence spending, with dogs among the first services to be cut. The dogs had been so valuable, however, that other countries had paid attention and by the start of World War II, the German Army had more than 20,000 fully trained war dogs. Britain again had to catch up and established a war dog school in a commandeered greyhound racing kennels at Potters Bar in 1942. This time the main dog in use was the German shepherd being widely known for its superior intelligence, stamina, loyalty and courage. It is still a popular military dog.

No history about British military dogs could be complete without mentioning on the Army Dog Unit Northern Ireland—ADU NI. It was established in 1973, only disbanding in 2007, making it the longest running deployment in the British Army. During the unit's existence it had expanded from a couple of handlers at the beginning to more than 100 in later years. Their successes included the capture of 21 major high-risk terrorists and 14 tonnes of arms and explosives.

The RAVC have dog trainers serving today in Cyprus, Germany, Brunei, Iraq, Afghanistan, mainland UK and Northern Ireland. I was on parade a few years back with a young lance corporal from the RAVC who had come to Australia on an ANZAC exchange posting for six months. He had already been to Iraq, Afghanistan, Northern Ireland and a UN posting in the former Yugoslavia. He had more medals at 22 than most soldiers get in a life time, such is the British Army's reliance and trust in sending dogs to war zones.

Some of the roles a young dog handler might face today include searching vehicles for explosives coming into camp, going out on patrol with an infantry detachment to track down the Taliban or walking in advance of a convoy looking for mines or roadside bombs.

The Royal Air Force dog unit has a long and rich history of its own, starting in 1942 under Lieutenant Hugh Bathurst-Brown in order to supply guard dogs within for airfields and aircraft production sites. Today the RAF dogs provide essential force protection to worldwide operations. RAF dogs are still used to guard facilities and also do everything mentioned that the RAVC handlers do. The RAF dogs have an incredible service record have served or currently in: Ghana, Singapore, Aden, Hong Kong, Northern Ireland, Falklands, Bosnia, Kosovo, Diego Garcia, Gibraltar, Cyprus, Kuwait, Saudi Arabia, Iraq and Afghanistan.

Austria ⭐》》

In Austria pack animals, due to the topography of the land, have always been on the order of battle for defence and to aid in rescue operations. The Austrian Army has a wealth of operational experience with pack animals dating back many hundreds of years, but was probably at its peak afterWorld War I and during World War II, under German command. When the Austrian army's specialist mountain troops—the Gebirgsjager—were absorbed into the Wehrmacht in 1939, they had large numbers of Haflinger horses and mules as key components of the regiments already. These very sure-footed horses had been bred and used in mountainous areas for pack missions. After World War II, these same pack horse units were reformed as part of the new Austrian Federal Army, they are still part of this force today.

Today these animals support the 6th Infantry Mountain Brigade, carrying the unit's ammunition, food and other supplies to positions high up in impassable terrain. A friend of mine was recently heli-skiing in Austria and had just been dropped off at several thousand feet into virgin powder. As the helicopter disappeared down towards the valley floor he heard a noise and looked around. To his amazement seven pack horses with an army reserve unit went trekking past him.

Haflingers are also a comfortable riding horse and are used by members of the mountain troop reconnaissance sections on patrols and liaison duties. These mounts have a quick turn of speed, ideal when patrols are tasked to support civilian authorities in border patrols. Many people try and cross the border illegally on foot and the horses give this mission to track them down an advantage of observation, terrain-crossing ability and speed. The horses work well at night and can traverse the many narrow paths off road vehicles cannot. They can also cross streams and other obstacles with ease compared to a vehicle.

The weather does not seem to worry them to much either. In 2009, when a group of people were trapped on a high mountain pass, the Black Hawk helicopter equipped with all the state of the art weather and rescue radar could not fly due to safety and other rescue vehicles' fuel had frozen in the low temperatures. The horses, however, made it and rescued all the people.

In the high mountains of Kosovo, the Austrian multinational peacekeeper force, insurgents and criminal smuggler elements all have one thing in common: they ride horses and use pack animals. In the poorly developed mountainous regions of the Balkans, with bad roads, bad weather and often no other means of transport, horses are still regularly used. The Austrian Army use their horses to supply UN observation posts in the mountain passes. Likewise in 2005 the Austrian forces intercepted whilst on mounted patrols a large convoy of 15 Kosovo Liberation Army fighters with 50 heavily laden pack animals carrying seven tonnes of ammunition.

Sadly no lessons were learnt from these missions and after the UN mission ceased in 2007, Austria reduced its 116 pack animals and some 47 horses by a third. There is still one pack company in the regular army and the Defence Department claims will be retained well into the future.

Of course horses are not the only animal in Austrian service. Dogs, like in neighbouring Switzerland, work in civilian search and rescue. Other dog roles include law enforcement by the Austrian military police who use their dogs in the guard and in the attack mode. Specialist military police dogs also work in explosive and narcotic detection dogs. The Austrian Army is quite small and the selection process to enter is very high. The military police dog section is renowned for having the highest selection standards of personnel.

Austria's military has used dogs as long as its pack horses. An article in a newspaper dated 25 November, 1887 stated:

For some time past the Austrian troops in Bosnia have been using dogs for military purposes. The animals are doing such good work that the War Minister has resolved to make a trial with them on a larger scale. During the winter, a number of dogs will be trained in patrol and outpost duty, so as to be able to take part in the autumn maneuvers next year.

Like the Haflinger horse, back in World War I, Austria used war dogs to haul small machine guns and equipment in mountainous terrain. When Germany annexed Austria at the beginning of World War II, all military dogs went to the

German Army. Today, the Austrian military dog teams have also found themselves assisting in border patrols since the collapse of the Soviet bloc. And far away from the snow a military police dog contingent patrols the UN separation zone between Syria and Israel.

War dogs have to be used to operating in all types of terrain be it desert, jungle or snow. Photograph courtesy of ADFTAWDA.

Argentina ⭐》》

Argentina, by virtue of its terrain, has a long association with mountain warfare and the use of animals.

Even today there are conflicts over mountainous territory with Chile. Horses and mules are used today by Argentina's Mountain and Forest Brigades, which are formed from two infantry and two cavalry regiments each. In addition they are supported by artillery and logistics units, making them a self-contain fighting force. These units are equipped with mules for transport and one of the cavalry units, the Lutaingo Squadron, and its supporting units uses horses, whilst the other cavalry unit designated simply RCM4 has light tanks and motocross bikes.

These horse squadrons are used to rapidly cross heavily forested areas that lack roads. They also have abundant rivers that can be quickly traversed by horse. Many of these men are trained snipers and dismount prior to any engagement.

These units are trained and equipped with the terrain in which they operate, such as mountains, heavily forested areas and high plateau deserts. They wear baggy camouflage pants with high lace-up riding boots and a camouflaged beret. They are ready to fight on the home front or outside their national borders, including Argentina's international commitments with United Nations Peace Keeping Forces.

To do this they rely on the military mule. They have two types of mules in their breeding program. Riding mules—a cross between a donkey and a light horse—are used by mounted infantry whilst pack mules—a cross between a donkey and the Percheron heavy horse—are used to carry heavy loads.

Mules are not new to this part of the world. They were of vital importance in commercial transportation during the colonial era and participated extensively in the War of Independence. In 1817, General Jose de San Martin with his Liberation army crossed the Andes Mountains bordering Chile with 5000 soldiers mounted on mules, with additional mules carrying artillery and supplies.

During World War I, the country supplied many thousands of mules to the US army. In the years before World War II, Argentine army officers were sent to Italy to take mule courses with the Alpine Brigade. One of them, Lieutenant Colonel Juan Peron, would latter on become three-time president of Argentina. Peron in fact wrote the first manual for the use of animals in mountain warfare.

In 1978, Argentina planned to invade Chile via the international passes of the Andes mountain range with Sherman Tanks. This proved an utterly foolish idea

'Camo' yourself but do not forget the horse. Just like vehicles, all forms of transport may need to be concealed. Photograph courtesy of Argentine Military Attaché Canberra.

given the terrain, so much so that when advised of the pending attack the Chileans army simply did not believe it. Today, the Argentinean planning may be more sophisticated and they even have units in modern tanks to fight at the foot of the mountains and in the valleys. But in the forests and high terrain, the mules and horse are still king.

Within the other parts of the army, there are also several independent equine units. One is the Fanfarria, which is a mounted band. The other is Regiminero de Grandaderos a Caballo General San Martin, which is similar to Britain's House Hold Cavalry in function. Finally there are several independent artillery groups that use pack mules. These units have four guns batteries instead of six due to peace time budget cuts. Each gun in turn is cut down to four loads. All up each battery requires 52 mules to carry ammunition and 12 mules to carry the gun parts.

The squadrons are named after battles fought by General Lavalle; El Hinojal and Bacacay. Bacacay is Argentina's last complete horse combat unit. Horses are used to rapidly cross hard terrain. The local mountains here are heavily forested and lack roads. There is also an abundance of mountain rivers that can be easily traversed on horseback but would take considerable operational engineer assets to cross by vehicles. The horses move in terrain not accessible by motor vehicle but are left at some distance from the enemy to avoid detection due to noise. This unit appears trained for conventional war and border patrol, but not for guerrilla warfare. The Ituzaingó Light Mountain Cavalry Squadron is also equipped as a tank/motorbike unit. Camacuá is a command/logistic unit with jeeps, trucks and inflatable boats.

The troops use FN FAL 7,62mm rifles. They wear baggy camouflage pants with high riding boots laced up front. Headwear is a French-like field cap and the usual Argentinean camouflage beret.

Jeff Isaacs

The Animals in War monument in London's Hyde Park

About The Author

Nigel Barry Allsopp was born in the United Kingdom started his military career as a military working dog handler in the Royal New Zealand Air Force Police in 1980. Within his 15 years' service, he rose to the rank of dogmaster responsible for all aspects of canine operations and training within the NZ Defence Force. During his service he was also a specialist narcotic detection dog handler and an explosive detection handler at various times. He conducted several operational tours of duty including Mogadishu in Somalia and United National postings which are still classified. He was the advisor to Special Forces on canine operations, including their use and evasion techniques. He became the first military dog trainer to qualify as a NZ Civilian Police dog trainer and supervisor.

Nigel has trained numerous government agencies such as Customs, Police, Corrective Service and Federal Aviation Security in the use of specialist dogs. Nigel has also trained and supplied specialist detection dogs and MWDs to South East Asian Countries on behalf of formal government requests whilst in the Defence

Deptartment. Nigel left the military to pursue a keen interest in wild canine research and worked for the Auckland Zoo training all sorts of exotic animals to enhance their behavioural enrichment. This included several years as an Elephant keeper whilst also training the zoo's sea lions, camels and ungulates to promote their natural behaviours. He has written several articles on behavioural enrichment of captive animals for international zoological Journals, including the *American Elephant Managers' Journal* and the *Australasian Zoological Journal*. He has held several positions with the Australasian Zoological Society as advisor to endangered marsupials, including field research, capture and reintroduction into the wild of native species.

Nigel moved to Australia to continue his interest in wild canines by working at several zoos and wildlife parks with manned wolves, timber wolves, dingoes and African Cape hunting dogs. Whilst the Supervisor of Currumbin Wildlife Sanctuary in Queensland, Australia, Nigel was been seconded to various zoos and wildlife parks as an advisor on animal enrichment management, including captive elephant management at Dubbo Zoo, NSW, marine mammal enrichment at SeaWorld Australia, and rhino management and dingo enrichment programs for Steve Irwin at Australia Zoo.

Nigel has appeared on several TV Wildlife programs such as Jack Hanna's and Steve Irwin's animal series. He was also a guest lecturer at Macquarie University on marsupial captive management and a speaker at several international zoo keeping conferences.

Nigel was the Training and Assessment Officer for the Box Hill TAFE, Victoria and Brisbane TAFE, Queensland in Zookeepers Certificate level III courses.

After a number of years in the wildlife industry the lure of working with dogs again caused Nigel to join the Queensland Police Service where he is currently a senior constable in the QPS Dog Section, both operating and training numerous specialist detection dogs for various government departments. Nigel continues to remain involved in K9 Organisations as the historian of the Australian Defence Force Trackers and War Dog Association. Nigel continues to be a saught-after guest speaker on both working dog and exotic animal training and management. His expertise has been sort on the use of equine transport by Special Force operations in mountainous terrain.

As a published author in the USA and Australasia, Nigel has written several books on war dogs and police dogs including the best sellers *Cry Havoc, Four Legged Diggers* and *K9 Cops*. Nigel has written numerous articles on canine training for international law enforcement magazines and has been a contributing author to the prestigious *British Royal Army Veterinary Corps Journal* and other military journals in the United States. He has been the canine subject matter expert on TVs *Mastermind*. He has also appeared on the TV series *Who Let the Dogs Out*. Nigel is a vocal ambassador for the establishment of animal memorials to recognise their role and contribution in all wars.

The War Animal's Prayer

Below is a prayer for the Remembrance of animals at War. The first verse was written by an anonymous poet known as "Sergeant 4486" from World War 1, the second verse by Julie Taylor-Radcliffe.

The glamour gone, some scattered graves and memories dim remain
With their old pals across a field, they'll never trek again
But yet there's nothing they regret as they await their call
For what was done or lost or won, they did their bit – that's all

Now as silent as the guns have fallen
Their tired hearts resting, closed eyes of loving grace
I ask in your quiet thoughts of Honourable Remembrance
You allow them, the animals to take their long awaited place.

Please in the silence of the hour spare some thought for this forgotten Army

"To love unconditionally, to serve unquestionably
To trust beyond endurance.
Bearing no malice, loyal and protective
They work, play, live, share, enrich, fight and die for us and with us, asking little in return.
They are the animals.
Oh that man could live by this creed also".

Julie Taylor-Radcliffe

DEDICATED TO ALL
WAR ANIMALS
THEY ALSO
SERVED

LEST WE FORGET

Bibliography

Books & Articles

Allsopp, N.B. Cry Havoc. New Holland Publications, 2011.

Administration in the Field. Army Code No.70182, 1966

Cooper, Jilly. Animals in War. London, 1983.

Hill, Anthony. Animal Heroes.

Gardiner, Juliet. The Animals of War. Portrait Books

Gasperini, W. "Uncle Sam's Dolphins," Smithsonian, pp. 28-29, September 2003.

Michelle Tan - Staff writer UK Defence News

Officers Pocket Book. Jun.1967

Royal Corps of Transport Training, A/26/GS Trg Pubs/2887

Sugarman, Martin. Zion Muleteers of Gallipoli. 2007

Websites

en.wikipedia.org/wiki/Australian_Light_Horse

en.wikipedia.org/wiki/Defence_Animal_Centre

en.wikipedia.org/wiki/War_animals

www.absoluteastronomy.com/

www.ansi.okstate.edu/

www.eurocbc.org/

www.fas.org/

www.globalsecurity.org/

www.marines.mil/news/Pages/

www.mca-marines.org/leatherneck/

www.militaryhorse.org/

www.olive-drab.com/

www.pigeonsincombat.com/

www.public.navy.mil/

www.squidoo.com/

First published in 2014 by New Holland Publishers Pty Ltd
London • Sydney • Cape Town • Auckland

The Chandlery Unit 114 50 Westminster Bridge Road London SE1 7QY United Kingdom
1/66 Gibbes Street Chatswood NSW 2067 Australia
Wembley Square First Floor Solan Road Gardens Cape Town 8001 South Africa
218 Lake Road Northcote Auckland New Zealand

www.newhollandpublishers.com

A record of this book is held at the British Library and the National Library of Australia.

ISBN 9781742575131

Managing Director: Fiona Schultz
Publisher: Alan Whiticker
Editor: Jason Mountney
Designer: Keisha Galbraith
Production Director: Olga Dementiev
Printer: Toppan Leefung Printing Ltd (China)

10 9 8 7 6 5 4 3 2 1

Keep up with New Holland Publishers on Facebook
www.facebook.com/NewHollandPublishers

UK £9.99
US $14.99